D0675317

It Is Fun Making Money

G.W. King Jr.

www.xulonpress.com

The Amway Independent Business Owner Compensation Plan (IBO Compensation Plan) offers monthly and annual bonuses that IBOs can earn in accordance with their contract with Amway. IBOs also may qualify for the AMWAY™ Growth Incentives Program (GI Program), a collection of discretionary programs separate from the IBO Compensation Plan and that can vary from year to year. IBO eligibility for the GI Program is at Amway's discretion. The GI Program is available only to IBOs in "good standing" and those whose conduct demonstrates high ethical and business standards aligned with the goals and objectives of Amway and its related businesses.

The average monthly Gross Income for "active" IBOs was $202. Approximately 46% of all IBOs were "active." U.S. IBOs were considered "active" in months in 2010 when they attempted to make a retail sale, or presented the Amway IBO Compensation Plan, or received bonus money, or attended an Amway or IBO meeting. If someone sustained that level of activity every month for a whole year, their annualized income would be $2,424. Of course, not every IBO chooses to be active every month. "Gross Income" means the amount received from retail sales, minus the cost of goods sold, plus monthly bonuses and cash incentives. It excludes all annual bonuses and cash incentives, and all non-cash awards, which may be significant. There may also be significant business expenses, mostly discretionary, that may be greater in relation to income in the first years of operation.

Following are approximate percentages of IBOs in North America who achieved the illustrated levels of success in the performance year ending August 31, 2010: Diamond 0.01%; Founders Diamond 0.01%; Executive Diamond and above 0.01%

For more details on qualifying for the GI Program and the requirements for good standing, see information on Amway.com or contact Amway Sales.

Lifestyle Disclosure: The success depicted in this profile may reflect income from sources other than Amway, such as earnings from the sale of training and education materials or other businesses and investments.

BSM#56837

DEDICATION

——◦◦◦——

    This book is dedicated to my mother-in-law, Anna Adams, and my godmother, Mildred Jones and in the memory of my parents, G.W. King Sr. and Edith King; my father-in-law, Charles W. Adams Sr.; and my godfather, Chuck Jones.

CONTENTS

—◦◦◦—

INTRODUCTION

—*∿∿*—

I am writing this book to record some of the lessons I have learned about success. Yes, it is great to have a lot of money, but if you are not happy, you cannot consider yourself successful. We have all heard and read about people who are wealthy but are not enjoying their lives. The key is not how much money you make but whether you are enjoying it and having fun. Each of us has to find out for ourselves what makes us happy. Without question, you are going to have problems in your life, experiences that will try to bring you down. Knowing how to handle these experiences is one of the factors that will determine your happiness. I am blessed to be able to handle my problems, and I'm happy to share a basic foundation of life that has helped me do so: First, I know that God is in control of my life. Things happen in life that I have no control over, but with God, all things are possible. Having a balance in the spiritual, social, physical, and mental areas of life has helped me be successful. This book gives examples of other principles that can help you achieve success.

Do you ever wonder why some people are successful in everything they do and some people are not? The answer can be found in the way both groups of people think and approach problems. Your attitude will determine your success in life, and if you learn how to relax and enjoy yourself, you'll be surprised at the rewards you'll reap. My wife, Edna, and I have learned how to have fun in everything we do. We have been married for 40 years, and our life together gets better every day. We have been financially free for more than 30 years, since August 20, 1981. It is nice being in control of our lives and not controlled by money or a job. We started our own independent Amway business in 1977 and, in three years, were financially free. Edna and I enjoy traveling together and have taken a week's vacation every month for the last 30 years. This book will show you some of the key elements for achieving a similar lifestyle or reaching the goals that will make you happy. I hope you and others will benefit by reading my story. I think you'll find that it really is "fun making money," and Edna says that it is "fun spending it, too."

Chapter 1

FAMILY

—◦◦◦—

As children, almost all of us were asked, "What do you want to be when you grow up?" And our answers were most likely influenced by the examples around us. I grew up in East St. Louis with a wonderful family and a hard-working father. With the given name General Wilson King Jr., it was inevitable that I would be a leader. My father was called G.W., so I was called G.W. Jr. Most people didn't know what the G.W. meant. I think Wilson was a family name, because in the 1800s, many Black families added family names as first or middle names. My father was a successful businessman who owned a roofing and siding company. He wore a suit and tie to work every day and taught me at an early age that appearance is important. We owned our home in a nice Black neighborhood. We were not rich, but I never worried about money.

My mother, Edith Pearson King, was a loving person. Most people called her Pal. She worked as an elevator operator at the Famous-Barr store in downtown St. Louis. My father would take me with him to pick her up from work when I was a boy. In the evenings, she would help me with my homework at the dining room table. Later, she became a social worker for the city. On the weekends, we often entertained her family. Mother's parents were Luther Pearson Sr. and Rosie Lee Muldrow Pearson Blair. They had eight children: Luther Jr., whom we called Bubba; Edith, my mother; Lillian, called Denny; Vivian, called Peaches; Carl; Catherine, called Sis; Muldrow; and Rosemary. Luther Sr. died in a hunting accident before I was born. Rosie later married Samuel Blair. Grandmother Rosie was a delightful person. Her favorite saying was "I am fine and dandy and sweet as candy."

Looking back, it seems as if my aunts Peaches and Denny were always at the house. They enjoyed playing bingo, Pokeno, and a board game called Bonanza. Aunt Peaches was married to William Johnson (Uncle Willie), a police officer. My birthday was the same as his, so we celebrated together. When I was a kid, he played Santa at Christmastime. Aunt Peaches drilled me on my manners—how to say thank you, yes sir, yes m'am, and please. To this day, I'm glad she took the time to see that I was polite. Aunt Denny was married to Claude Bush, who was a minister. Because they had kids my age, I spent a lot of time at their home. She loved to cook, and there was always a lot of food.

I was born 15 years after my two sisters, Yvonnejenai, whom we call Nana, and Fayetta Jean, called Jean. They were in high school when I was born, so I grew up like an only child. My sisters called my parents Buddy Daddy and Mama Pal. Nana went on to be a laboratory technician, and Jean, a schoolteacher. Nana married Robert Robinson and had a daughter, Vivian, whom we call Cherry. I'm only four years older than my niece. Later, Nana and Robert divorced, and Cherry stayed with us when Nana moved to Cleveland. I remember having to take Cherry with me to the movie theater, about a block from our house. Back then, going to the movies was an all-day event, with two shows.

My sister Jean married Kenneth McKinney. As an example of the kind of man my father was, he built them a house on the lot behind our house. Jean and Kenneth had a daughter, Andrea. I was about nine years old when they first brought Andrea home from the hospital, and I thought she was the prettiest baby in the world.

Although he didn't finish high school, my father was perhaps the greatest influence in my life. Daddy played clarinet in a band and started in business with a gas station. He knew how to build friendships with people and was active in politics. In the 1950s and 60s, he was a Black leader of the Republican Party in East St. Louis. Back then, East St. Louis was mostly White and had been voted a Model City. Illinois was known as the land of Abe Lincoln, and since Lincoln was a Republican and had freed the slaves, there were a lot of Blacks in the Republican Party.

My father started a small roofing and siding company. His company also built some homes, but his biggest jobs were repairing school roofs for the city. He paid his employees with cash every Friday. I can remember the dining room table being full of money. Daddy had a license to carry a gun, and every Friday, I watched as he strapped it on. He ran the house just like a business, which meant that everyone got paid with cash in a small envelope. My chores consisted of taking out the trash and cutting the grass. I always looked forward to getting paid on Friday.

Even after I went to college, I came home every summer and worked for my father. I worked on a tar truck as we repaired school roofs. As you can imagine, it was a hot and sticky job. My father always told me to get an education so that I would not have to do that type of work full time. His advice and my experiences over the summer made me ready to go back to college. One summer, I got a job working for the Illinois highway department with the help of Bud Smith, one of the few Black engineers in the department at the time. Bud is the brother of Mildred Jones, my godmother. My godparents, Chuck and Mildred Jones, were my parents' best friends. Chuck was always the first person to enter our house on January 1st, and his wife made delicious pineapple pies.

Among the many things that I remember about my father is the fact that he always carried a lot of keys; when he came in the house, you could hear him. He worked six days a week and went to church on Sunday. He drove a station wagon, because he could carry tools in the back, and took me to work on Election Day. He always had a wad of money rolled up with a rubber band because it was too big for a regular money clip. Daddy liked cigars, but my mother didn't like smoke, so he just chewed on them. I never saw him smoke one. He reached the level of 33rd degree in the Masonic Lodge. When I turned 21, he asked me to join, and I became a 3rd degree Mason.

In the 1960s, with the start of the civil rights movement and the migration of Whites out of East St. Louis, real estate prices fell, and my father started buying property in the area. He went to night school to get his GED and his real estate broker's license. I remember doing my homework at one end of the dining room table and my father studying at the other end. Some of the property he bought after receiving his broker's license is still in the family. As a provider, he took care of both his own children and his children's children.

When I turned 16, I got my driver's license and was given a Pontiac Tempest. My father put me in charge of running errands for my grandmother Josephine Smith King. Grandmother King lived about two miles from us with her daughter Emma Lue, whom we called Sister. Her husband, Frank King, died when I was a child; my only memories of him are as a man sick in bed. Frank and Josephine had four children: my father; Frankie, whom we called Sweeten; Emma Lue; and Irene. Grandmother King called my father frequently for trips to the store; now I was her official driver. I often bought her King Edward cigars, which she smoked in the bathroom. Apparently, the family had made a deal with her to smoke cigars in the bathroom instead of dipping snuff.

My sister Jean's second husband was Ernie Page, a high school teacher and basketball coach. Jean had moved out of the house behind ours, so my cousin Faye Bush Tharp and her husband, Harry, moved in. It was great having them in the rear house, and they were a great influence on my life. I was in junior high, and the two of them taught me how to dance.

In 1977, the TV series *Roots* sparked a sense of Black pride across the country; families started having reunions and researching their heritage. In June of that year, my mother's family had scheduled a reunion in Cleveland, and I volunteered to document the family history so that it would be available at the reunion. The booklet I produced was called "Directory of the Descendants of Cooper and Emma Muldrow."

Of course, personal computers weren't available, so the best source for genealogical information was the U.S. Archives. My wife and I were living in Washington, DC, at the time, and we were able to go to the Archives in the evenings to do research. The work was tough on me mentally, because I had not thought of my ancestors as being slaves. As I read through Census information, I found my great-grandparents, Cooper and Emma Muldrow, the parents of my grandmother Rosie. They had lived in Muldrow, Mississippi, which was near Starkville. Cooper was born into slavery in 1854 and was the son of the slave owner William C. Muldrow. His mother was a 15-year-old slave named Marie Hampton (who later married Thomas Speed). Cooper had light skin and was listed as a Mulatto in the Census. He was educated and became the local postmaster and owned a small grocery store.

James English Cousar Jr., a descendant of the White side of the Muldrow family, published a book entitled *Physician Turned Planter*, documenting the journey of his side of the family from Ireland to America. I was curious to know what part of Africa my ancestors were from, so I had a DNA test conducted that traces ancestry back from mother to mother. The DNA test showed that my mother's family came from the Cameroon, West Africa, and the tribes of the Tikar, Mafa, and Hide peoples. Coincidentally, one of my cousins, Muldrow Callaway, had lived in the Cameroon for some years. The Tikar tribe made him a chief, and he changed his name to Fai Sum. I was astonished to learn that the tribe members somehow felt that he was a part of their family. After I received the DNA test results, I called Fai Sum, who now lives in the United States. He told me that he had already had the same DNA test done, and the results were the same, as we might expect, given that his grandmother was my great-grandmother. With the help of my aunt Frankie Griggs, I had a similar test done to trace the ancestry of my grandmother on my father's side of the family. The results showed that my father's ancestors had come from the Fulani peoples of Nigeria, Mali, and Guinea-Bissau.

Chapter 2

EDUCATION

———

From an early age, I was taught the importance of getting an education in order to get a good job. But in grade school, I had a stuttering problem. It was hard for me to stand up in class and speak, and I remember taking special speech classes. I think I grew out of stuttering when I reached Hughes Quinn Junior High School. I was only a C student, but I was good in math. Like my father, I played running back in junior high and made the football team, but I wasn't a starter. As I moved onto Lincoln High School, I learned how to study. I was now a B student, and my best subjects were drafting, math, and science. I tried out for the football team as a running back. The line coach, George Holiday, talked to me about becoming a guard, but I was only 5'7" and 165 pounds. I wasn't sure that I was big enough. The coach told me that with my speed and being low to ground, the position would work out well. The first week, my nose was broken, which made me mad. I did, however, make the team as a back-up, and by the second year, I was starting guard. In my senior year, I was co-captain of the team, and we had a winning season. I was even given an honorable mention in the St. Louis newspaper. I owe a great deal to my head coach,

Richard Brooks, who is married to my cousin Brenda Bush Brooks. I have been fortunate to have some great mentors throughout my life.

In high school, my best subject was math. My father mentioned that I should be an engineer or an architect because I was also good in drafting classes. My best design was a circular home that revolved by motor. I decided that civil engineering would be my line of study. In this career, I would design and build bridges and buildings. I also wanted to be in the military, so I checked out the military academies. My father used his political contacts to get me appointments as an alternate candidate to the Air Force Academy and West Point, but neither came through. I visited Southern Illinois University in Carbondale and liked the campus. My father reached out again to some of his political contacts, especially Senator Everett Dirksen, to get me a scholarship.

SIU had a large and beautiful campus about 20,000 students, 2,000 of them Black. During the week, I didn't see many Black students, but I found them at the weekend parties. Growing up in East St. Louis, I had not been acquainted with many Whites. Up until college, all my schools were all Black. I would see Whites when I went downtown but not many in my neighborhood. This was common in the late 1950s, but I didn't have a problem adjusting to the college and its largely White student population. My roommate in the dorm was White, and he and I got along fine.

On the weekends, I went to parties held by Black fraternities and sororities. I decided to pledge Omega Psi Phi, because that fraternity seemed unique. There were a lot of Kappas and Alphas on campus, but only six Omegas, five from New York City and one from Chicago. At every party, it seemed like the others were just waiting for the Omegas to arrive. After I pledged, I realized that two of my favorite relatives were in the fraternity: my cousin Richard Brooks, who had been my high school football coach, and my uncle Otis D. Morgan Sr., who was married to my father's sister Irene. After joining the fraternity, I became its leader—local basileus—and the next year, we recruited many more pledges. I even won the Sigma Gamma Rho sorority sweetheart contest, mostly because some of Omega's pledges were dating the sorority sisters. I introduced my cousin Gordon D. Bush to a Sigma Gamma Rho sister named Brenda, who later became his wife. Gordon went on to become the mayor of East St. Louis.

I enjoyed the engineering school and studied hard to get good grades. I learned how to study with some of the Ethiopian students, who were very smart. In my last year at SIU Carbondale, I met Edna and her sister Dorothy at a party on campus. They seemed like nice young ladies, but Edna wasn't dancing or having fun. I went over and started talking to her. When I told her that my name was G.W. King, and she asked, "What does the G.W. stand for?" But when I told her General Wilson, she didn't seem to believe me. Although I didn't know it at the time, if Edna wasn't interested in a young man, she would sometimes give out a fake name and phone number. I guess she thought I was playing the same game, and she relaxed, thinking that she wouldn't hear from me again. I got her real name and phone number and decided to call her for a date the next weekend. When her mother answered and I told her that General Wilson King was calling, I could hear her tell Edna, "There's some general on the phone." I picked Edna up for our date in Murphysboro, a rural town of about 9,000 people, six miles from Carbondale. As I turned off the main street into Edna's neighborhood, I was going so fast that I couldn't avoid hitting a deep pothole that almost tore up my car.

I enjoyed meeting Edna's family. She was the oldest of 12 children still living at home. Her father, Charles Adams, worked for the state wildlife department. He loved to hunt and fish and made sure his family always had a freezer full of fish and rabbits. Edna's mother, Anna, made me feel welcome. At the time, Edna was an LPN and contributed her earnings to help support the family. That made a good impression on me. We dated for about six months before I graduated from SIU with a B.S. in civil engineering.

After I graduated, my cousin Shedd Smith encouraged me to go to Washington, DC, to study at George Washington University. Shedd was a senior manager in the federal government and had received his master's degree in city planning. He told me about a work fellowship available for Blacks in city planning and said that with my degree in civil engineering, I would be a good candidate for the program. I applied and was accepted to the two-year master's degree program in urban and regional planning at GW. The program paid all university fees and allowed me to work part-time with the DC government. I was delighted to be able to go to school full-time and work part-time to earn some money to live on.

I found a one-room apartment near the university at 21st Street and Pennsylvania Avenue. With the White House just a few blocks away on 16th Street, I felt like a neighbor of the President. My cousin Shedd and his wife, Ingeborg, lived within walking distance in a beautiful apartment building next to the famous Watergate complex. It was nice to have relatives to show me around town, and I could walk to the Kennedy Center, the White House, and Georgetown.

Although I had driven my Pontiac Tempest to DC, I had to park several blocks away from my apartment and usually used it only on the weekends. I later met an older couple, Otis and Mattie Johnson, who allowed me to park in front of their house and agreed to keep an eye on my car during the week. Edna and I built a strong friendship with Otis and Mattie, who often invited us over to eat fried catfish or pork chops. When Otis passed away, we helped Mattie move into a senior citizen home.

Growing up in East St. Louis, my family had attended Mt. Zion Baptist Missionary Church. My father was a trustee, and I enjoyed Sunday school. I accepted Jesus Christ as my savior at an early age and was baptized by Reverend Rouse Sr. Later, the reverend's son, John H. Rouse, became pastor of the church. While I was at SIU, I attended the Rock Hill Baptist Church in Carbondale and taught Sunday school during my four years in college. Now, after arriving in DC in September 1970, I was looking for a church to attend.

Some of my co-workers in the DC government had recommended some local churches. I got up early one Sunday, intending to visit one of the churches on my list, but I couldn't find it. As I was driving, I saw another Baptist church that I decided to check out instead. This was the 10th Street Baptist Church, with a Sunday school class held upstairs in the balcony. That Sunday, I met both the Sunday school teacher, Dorothy Jones, and the pastor, John Thomas Jennings Sr. I didn't think about joining right away, because I still had a list of other churches to visit, but the next week, Mrs. Jones called and invited me to come back. I agreed and have now been a member at 10th Street Baptist for 40 years. That's a good lesson about the power of a follow-up phone call!

Through the years, a new church was built. After Pastor Jennings passed away, Reverend A. Michael Charles Durant became our new pastor. Pastor Durant and his wife, Kimberly, have done a great job in their roles as spiritual leaders. After services, Edna and I always find Dorothy Jones and Lucy Savage and give them a big hug. We have many other good friends from church, including Lonnie and Gail Johnson. Lonnie is now the pastor of the Ebenezer Baptist Church in DC, and his son Micah is our godson.

My first year at George Washington went by fast. Professor Dorn McGrath was the head of the urban and regional planning department and served as my mentor. I studied hard and got As and Bs in my classes. During the Christmas holidays, I asked Edna to marry me. She accepted, and we set our wedding date for September 5, 1971, the same day as my sister Jean's birthday. When I visited Aunt Frankie's home in Madison, IL, that year, she asked me if I had planned out my budget. I think she wanted to make sure I had enough money to get married. We wrote down a list of money coming in and money going out, and fortunately, it looked like I had enough to support us.

My fraternity brothers gave me a bachelor party the night before the wedding, but it wasn't an all-male party; both men and women attended. Still, I had a hangover on the day of my wedding. Edna and I were married at her church, Mt. Gilead Baptist Church in Murphysboro, IL. Both sets of parents paid for the wedding, and my parents gave us a honeymoon in Freeport, Bahamas. We had a great week there before coming home to Washington.

Edna and I started our new life together in a one-bedroom apartment furnished with hand-me-downs. We had enough money for our bills and to pay the tuition for Edna to attend Howard University. Edna was an LPN, but she wanted to get her bachelor's degree and become an RN. The next year went by fast, and before I knew it, I had my master's degree in urban and regional planning. I was offered a job with the DC government just at the time that the planning of the DC metro system got underway.

Chapter 3

LET'S TRAVEL THE WORLD

———∾∾∾———

Our honeymoon trip to the Bahamas sparked a dream in me to travel the world. I set a goal to go around the world in the next five years and then write a book about our travels. You might ask how I planned to achieve that dream with a full-time job and my wife as a full-time college student, but I've learned that when the dream is big enough, the facts don't count. Over the next five years, Edna and I traveled around the world, and in 1977, I published a book entitled *Our World Travels and Adventures: The Experiences of a Young Black Couple.* I kept records of all of our travels from September 1971 to October 1976, documenting every trip we took, including business trips to study transportation systems, vacations, graduations, weddings and funerals. Although that earlier book is now out of print, it sold well at the time, and I have summarized some of its contents in this chapter. I include stories of some of our travels in the United States, Europe, Russia, Mexico, South America, the Orient, West Africa, Canada, and on a cruise in the Caribbean.

One of our first trips was to San Francisco. A planning convention was being held there, and I talked my supervisors into sending me. The government paid for my ticket, hotel room, and a small allowance for living expenses. I bought Edna a student ticket, and we were off to California. My mother gave me the names and phone numbers of some relatives in San Francisco, and she advised me to visit them around 5:00 p.m. so that they would invite us to stay for dinner. We took her advice and were happily fed by each of them.

After the convention, Edna and I stayed a few extra days to sightsee and relax. We visited the downtown area, Chinatown, and Fisherman's Wharf and took pictures of the Golden Gate Bridge. Neither of us had ever seen hills as steep as they were in San Francisco, especially Lombard Street, the most crooked street in the city. On our last night, we decided to splurge and eat dinner at a nice restaurant. We settled on one straight up a hill about three blocks from our hotel. I had $20 in my pocket, which I thought would be enough to pay for our meal, but when we sat down and looked at the menu, we realized we didn't have enough money. An inexperienced traveler, I had left my traveler's checks in the hotel room. I told Edna to stay at the restaurant while I went back to the hotel to get the traveler's checks. Of course, when I reached the room, the checks were locked in the suitcase and Edna had the key! At that point, I could either break open the suitcase–but it was the only one we owned—or carry it back up the hill to the restaurant. When I walked back into the restaurant carrying the suitcase, I said, "I sure hope you all take traveler's checks." After such a fiasco, Edna and I had a delicious meal and made a toast to our happiness.

OUR FIRST TRIP TO EUROPE

Part of the reason I wanted to see the world was to be

able to study global transportation systems. At this time in our lives, I was working full-time, and Edna was going to Howard University to get her degree in nursing. To earn comp time that would allow us to travel, I worked almost every weekend.

In May 1972, while Edna was on summer break, we took our first big international trip for two weeks to Europe. We found some cheap airline tickets and were off, armed with the book *Europe on $5.00 a Day*. We were fortunate to have some friends, Tony and Cynthia Marshall, who lived in West Berlin, so we made that our first stop. Tony was a sergeant in the U.S. Air Force and Cynthia worked on the military base. They had a car and both spoke German. Edna and I stayed with Tony and Cynthia in their apartment, and they took us sightseeing all over West Berlin, including a stop at Checkpoint Charlie at the Berlin Wall. We then purchased a train pass and traveled to Paris. Our travel book guided us to a nice hotel near the Arc de Triomphe in the Champs Elysees area. Riding the Paris metro system, we saw the Cathedral of Notre-Dame, Montmarte, the opera area, and of course, the Eiffel Tower, which we ascended for a beautiful view of the city.

The three-hour train ride from Paris to Brussels, Belgium, was smooth and scenic. We stayed near the Grand Place in a small hotel for $5.00 a night. The Grand Place is a huge square enclosed by Gothic buildings. It is one of Europe's most beautiful public squares, with a colorful flower market, quaint restaurants, and specialty shops along the street. One afternoon, we rode public transit to the National African Art Museum in the suburbs. After two relaxing days in Brussels, we next visited Amsterdam. Fifty miles of canals divide this city into 70 islands, which are connected by 500 bridges. Our sightseeing included the Rijksmuseum (with an outstanding collection of Dutch art), the Ann Frank House, the Artis Zoo, the Rembrandt House, and a canal cruise in a glass-topped boat.

From Amsterdam, we flew to London, where we stayed in the Grand Hotel near Russell Square and the British Museum. Although most of our sightseeing was done on the London subway, we took a bus tour of the city that included Westminster Abbey (London's greatest Gothic church), the Tower of London, Buckingham Palace, St. James's Palace, Hyde Park, No. 10 Downing Street, the west end commercial district, and Piccadilly Circus (an entertainment area similar to Times Square in New York City). The trip to Europe was a great experience for both of us and whet our appetites to see more of the world.

NIAGARA FALLS AND TORONTO, CANADA

For our first wedding anniversary in September 1972, Edna and I drove to Niagara Falls and Toronto, Canada. In Niagara Falls, we stayed at a nice, inexpensive motel about two miles from the Falls. We spent most of our time visiting the area's attractions, including the antique auto museum, the floral clock, Whirlpool Rapids, Table Rock House (with an elevator that descends for a close-up of the Canadian Horseshoe Falls and the Niagara River), and the Whirlpool Aero car (a cable car that carries passengers high over the whirlpool basin), and of course, we admired the beautiful Niagara Falls. One evening, we played miniature golf and went out for dinner. We also spent a day in Toronto, about a two-hour drive from Niagara Falls. There, we rode the subway and visited the new city hall. The city hall was a striking complex consisting of a three-story domed rotunda framed by two slender towers, one tower with 27 floors and the other with 20 floors. During lunch hour, a band played in the mall area in front of city hall. A huge fountain was also located in the mall, which is converted into an ice-skating rink during the winter.

EUROPE AND RUSSIA

Our next trip to Europe was in 1973 for three weeks with a group of about 30 engineers and city planners. The trip was sponsored by the Metropolitan Association of Urban Designers and Environmental Planners (MAUDEP). Edna and I were joined on the trip by my mother, Edith, and her sister Peaches. Our group leaders were Bob and Eva Schumacher. I had registered for the trip under my full name (General Wilson King Jr.), and Bob and Eva were slightly surprised upon our arrival because they were expecting a military general. Our itinerary included one night in Amsterdam, five nights in Moscow, five nights in Leningrad, four nights in Paris, and six nights in London. We spent more money in the first two days than we had on our entire last trip to Europe.

Tours and meetings were planned throughout the day during our visit to Moscow. We saw Red Square, a panoramic view of the Kremlin, Moscow University, the famous Bolshoi Opera House, and Lenin Stadium. We spent one morning touring the Kremlin area, which consisted of a number of beautiful cathedrals. We visited one of the Kremlin museums, where everyone was required to wear cloth shoe covers over their shoes. The museum held the jewels and clothing of the czars. The MAUDEP group also attended an urban planning exhibition (which included demonstration models of Soviet housing construction) and took a tour of the Moscow subway. It was remarkable to see such an elegant subway station, with sculptures, paintings, and chandeliers.

We flew Soviet Airlines from Moscow to Leningrad (now St. Petersburg) and stayed at the Hotel Leningrad, located on the river. Leningrad has many canals, lending the city a very pleasant atmosphere. The MAUDEP group took a sightseeing tour of the city that included the Peter and Paul Fortress, the Hermitage (one of the world's most famous museums), Palace Square, and Moskovsky Prospekt (a main street with shops and offices).

The group also had a meeting with the Leningrad metro officials, who explained their system and took us on a tour of the subway. The most remarkable subway line had stations that simulated a lobby with several elevator doors. The trains were hidden behind the walls and the train doors lined up with the doors in the station.

One of the most fantastic sights in Russia was the summer palace of the czars, Petrodvorets, located about 30 miles from Leningrad on the Bay of Finland. The complex actually consisted of two palaces, a large palace (now a museum) and a small one on the bay. The area also featured more than 100 beautiful water fountains.

We next flew to Paris and stayed in a small hotel in the Champs Elysees area. Again, we did most of our sightseeing by subway. Since Edna and I had visited Paris before, we showed Mother and Aunt Peaches around the city. We took another trip to the top of the Eiffel Tower; saw the Cathedral of Notre-Dame, the opera area, the Arc de Triomphe, and the Louvre (the world's richest museum); and took a half day trip to Versailles (the palace of Louis XIV, which includes beautiful gardens and fountains). With the MAUDEP group, we took a tour of the Paris subway, met with Paris metro planners, and visited some of the newer metro stations. The group also took a unique tour of the sewers of Paris. In the evening, we saw a show at the Folies Bergere and took a night tour of the city on a double-decker bus.

Our last stop on this trip was London, where my mother and Aunt Peaches had a wonderful time. We took a sightseeing tour that included Westminster Abbey, the Tower of London, St. James's Palace, No. 10 Downing Street, and the House of Parliament. The next morning, we watched the changing of the guard at Buckingham Palace and, in the evening, visited Piccadilly Circus. One of the most memorable experiences of the trip was Aunt Peaches's telephone call from Scotland Yard to the East St. Louis police station. Her husband, William Johnson, was a police captain in East St. Louis and was thrilled to receive a call from Scotland Yard.

MEXICO

For our next trip, we had planned to travel to South America, but I found a nice tour to Mexico that I couldn't pass up. The United Buyers Service offered a round-trip flight to Mexico for $149 per person. The flight would leave Washington, DC, for Mexico City, with a flight back to Washington from Acapulco. For another $100 per person, we received land accommodations (first-class hotels, bag transfers, and bus transportation from Mexico City to Taxco and Acapulco). In May of 1974, then, we took off to spend three nights in Mexico City, one night in Taxco, and three nights in Acapulco.

Our first hotel was modern and clean, but the elevators had almost continuous problems. At the hotel, we met

Felix, a student at the University of Mexico. We were happy to hire Felix as our tour guide; he charged $5.00 per person for a full-day tour of the city in his car and came recommended by the hotel staff. Edna and I were joined on this tour by three young ladies. Together, we saw the Xochimilco Floating Gardens (boats covered with flowers that traveled down a beautiful canal), the National Palace, the Guadalupe Shrine, Chapultepec Park (with its beautiful fountains), the Museum of Anthropology (where the original Aztec calendar is housed), the University of Mexico (bedecked with mosaic murals almost large as the buildings themselves), and Zocalo (Mexico City's main plaza). The next afternoon, Felix drove us 30 miles outside of Mexico City for some shopping and to visit the Pyramids of Teotihuacan, dating back 2,000 years. The pyramids of the sun and moon were quite a sight. I, along with some others, climbed 200 feet to the top of the pyramid, where I truly felt like a King! Mexico City's modern subway system was also a convenient and efficient means of travel around the city.

The tour group left Mexico City by bus to travel to Taxco with a stop in Cuernavaca, where we passed the home of the actor Paul Newman. As we approached the "Silver City" of Taxco, we drove through winding hills and could see Mexicans riding burrows, sporting colorful blankets. Taxco is a silver-mining town located in the mountains about 110 miles south of Mexico City. The town's streets are narrow and made of cobblestone. The center of town featured numerous silver shops selling silver rings, bracelets, and necklaces, as well as the Church of Santa Prisca and Sebastian, one of Mexico's finest and most beautifully appointed churches.

The next day, the bus tour traveled to Acapulco, known

for its beautiful beaches and relaxing atmosphere. We spent most of our time there either on the beach or in the hotel's swimming pool. The main attraction was the world-famous La Perla cliff-divers, who plunged into the water at more than 60 mph. We had a brief sightseeing tour of the downtown area and the beautiful coastline. One evening, we had dinner at the Crazy Lobster restaurant, which offered a romantic atmosphere and delicious food. Our impression of Acapulco was a combination of magnificent scenery with the comforts of a modern city. It is a place for both relaxation and romance.

SOUTH AMERICA

In August 1974, only thee months after our trip to Mexico, Edna and I planned to spend a week in Caracas, Venezuela, along with my parents, Edith and G.W. Since my family had given us our honeymoon trip to the Bahamas, Edna and I thought it would be nice to treat my parents to a second honeymoon. My niece Cherry paid for my father's ticket, and Edna and I bought my mother's. Mother and Dad flew to Washington, DC, a few days prior to our departure for South America. Our tour was for three nights on the beach at Macuto and four nights in the city of Caracas.

We stayed at the Macuto Sheraton on the Caribbean coast of Venezuela. The view from our hotel room was breathtaking, with mountains sloping down to the sea. It was fascinating to watch the white clouds dip below the mountains. We could see miles of golden, sandy beaches and beautiful tropical gardens. The hotel atmosphere was like paradise. After four days at the beach, we were transported by taxi to Caracas (about 40 minutes away), a picturesque city surrounded by mountains. There, we saw soaring glass and chrome skyscrapers side by side with quaint Spanish colonial buildings. We stayed at the Tamanaco Intercontinental Hotel, which was situated on a lush green hill amid 39 acres of tropical gardens. The hotel boasted restaurants, a bar, a pool, tennis courts, and a gym and sauna. Our room overlooked the swimming pool and a beautiful view of the city.

Mother, Dad, Edna, and I were eager to take the red cable car to the top of Mt. Avila. The ride cost only 50 cents and offered a panoramic view of the city and the sparkling Caribbean, 7,000 feet below. From the top of Mt. Avila, you could take another cable car down the other side of the mountain to Macuto. During our stay, we toured the old city of Caracas, with the Casa Natal (the birthplace of Simon Bolivar, the liberator of Venezuela and many South American nations); the beautiful Santa Capilla with its ornate altar; the National Pantheon (where Bolivar is buried); and the Plaza Bolivar. We also attended a bullfight in the old Nuevo Circo Bullring, where Spanish matadors match their skill against the bulls. On the evening after the bullfight, we decided to go see a movie and then have dinner. I called a taxi and showed the driver the address of the movie theater from an English newspaper. The driver didn't speak English, but from the price he indicated, we knew that the theater couldn't be too far away. When we reached our destination after about 15 minutes, we were surprised to find ourselves at a drive-in theater! We had a good laugh along with the driver and asked him to take us to a restaurant for dinner. Our visit to Caracas was made all the more enjoyable by seeing Mother and Dad having so much fun.

EDNA'S GRADUATION GIFT: A TRIP TO THE ORIENT

Edna received her bachelor of science degree in nursing from Howard University in May of 1975. For this joyous occasion, we planned a royal celebration. Our family chartered a 40-seat, double-decker bus and traveled to Washington from East St. Louis. What a wonderful treat it was to have the family in Washington to celebrate Edna's graduation! Our cousin Shedd Smith gave a party in the ballroom of his apartment complex. The family weekend visit really made Edna's graduation a grandiose event. My graduation present to Edna was a trip to the Orient that included the following cities: Las Vegas; Los Angeles; Anchorage, Alaska (a brief refueling stop); Tokyo, Kyoto, and Osaka, Japan; Taipei, Taiwan (in the Republic of China); Hong Kong; and Honolulu.

Our adventure started with a flight to Las Vegas, where we learned that everything we had ever heard about the city was true. First of all, it is definitely the entertainment capital of the world. The city offered a number of shows featuring top entertainers, although gambling is the main attraction. The hotels and casinos try to outdo one another with spectacular gambling and entertainment that goes on 24 hours a day. Our two-day visit put Las Vegas on the list of our favorite places.

The next stop on our tour was Los Angeles, where Edna and I stayed with my cousins Rosella and Jimmy Spencer. After three days of sightseeing in LA, we headed for the Orient. Our "non-stop" flight to Tokyo actually stopped twice, once in San Francisco and once in Anchorage, where the temperature was 70 degrees, but the city was surrounded by snow-capped mountains. Our flight from

Anchorage to Tokyo took six hours.

Tokyo, Japan

In Tokyo, we stayed at the Imperial Hotel, which was in the center of the city and very comfortable. Across from our hotel was the impressive Habiya Park, with its beautiful fountains. The view from the top of the Tokyo Tower was one of the most fantastic sights we saw. Tokyo Tower is 1,100 feet tall (50 feet taller than the Eiffel Tower), the highest point from which to view the city. The Ginza area was equally fascinating; at night, this district comes alive with neon lights, similar to Times Square in New York City.

Kyoto, Japan

Edna and I took a morning flight from Tokyo to Kyoto that offered a majestic view of the snow-capped Mount Fuji, the highest mountain in Japan. Kyoto was the classic capital of Japan for ten centuries. We stayed at the Kyoto Grand Hotel, which was centrally located and very comfortable. Our tour of the city included the Gold Pavilion, a Buddhist temple that was once the residence of a governor. The Gold Pavilion made a beautiful reflection in a nearby lake. We also toured Nijo Castle, the former residence of the Tokugawa clan, who ruled Japan for centuries. The so-called "nightingale floor" of the castle was designed to make an odd sound when visitors walked on it to warn against any intruders who might try to assassinate the *shogun* (emperor). Among our other stops was the famous Kiyomizu Temple, with its rock garden, and the Shinmonzen Street shopping area. We also attended a traditional Japanese art show at Gion Corner. The show featured flower arrangements, Japanese music and dancing, a *bunraku* performance (a kind of puppet show), and the tea ceremony.

Osaka, Japan

Edna and I took the bullet train (the fastest train in the world, which travels up to 135 mph) from Kyoto to Osaka. Osaka is about 30 miles from Kyoto, and it took us about 17 minutes to make the trip. The ride was smooth and comfortable.

Osaka is Japan's second largest city, with a population at the time of more than 3 million people. It is regarded as Japan's most important commercial and industrial center. When we arrived at the Osaka train station, I telephoned a friend, Hiroski Sato, a transportation planner from Osaka who had visited my planning office in Washington. Sato met us at the train station and, from there, took us to some unique subway stations. He also treated us to a delicious lunch and a tour of his office, the Osaka Municipal Transportation Bureau. I met the director, and the two of us discussed some of the transportation problems in Osaka. Sato took us in a chauffeured car to see some of the city's highway projects and tourist attractions. We visited both the Osaka Castle and the Tsutenkaku Tower. The Osaka Castle is a replica of a castle built by Toyotomi Hideyoshi in 1586 that was subsequently twice destroyed by fire. The Tsutenkaku Tower is a postwar version of an older tower that was dismantled during the war. It is more than 300 feet high (twice as high as the castle) and offered an impressive view of the city. We traveled back to Kyoto that evening on the regular train; although it wasn't as fast as the bullet train, it featured a TV that allowed us to watch sumo wrestling as we traveled back to Kyoto.

Taipei, Taiwan

Our next stop was Taipei, Taiwan, in the Republic of China. We had an evening flight to Taipei, and our tour agent had arranged a car to take us to the Presidential Hotel. The hotel was located in the center of the city, and our large room featured a TV, but because very few programs were broadcast in English, I mostly watched baseball games. Our tour in Taipei included the 200-year-old Longshan Temple; the National Historical Museum, with its ancient jade, bronze, painted scrolls, and books brought over from mainland China; Presidential Square; the Handcraft Promotion Center, where you could buy jade, coral, and pottery; and the city business and theater district.

We were fortunate to have another friend, Chung-Yi Hsueh, who lived in the city of Taipei. Hsueh is a transportation planner who had worked with me for six months in Washington. He came over to the hotel and took us all around the city. We did most of our touring by bus, which included a ride to a beautiful park on the top of a mountain. The view of the city and landscape gardening was fantastic from the top of the mountain. On our way down from the mountain park, we stopped at the College of Chinese Culture, where Hsueh had been a student.

We also spent one day in the northern portion of the island of Taiwan. Hsueh was able to get a taxi to drive us around all day for about $15.00. Our visit to the northern portion of the island included the city of Chilung (where the harbor is located), the beautiful beach area, and a few

Buddha statues. One of the most unique sights was a beach area consisting of rock formations shaped like human heads. Having a friend in Taipei enabled us to see many areas that the average visitor wouldn't know about. Hsueh showed us a fantastic time in Taipei.

Hong Kong

Edna and I had a morning flight from Taipei to Hong Kong. As the plane landed, our eyes captured a beautiful view of the city, surrounded by blue waters and mysterious mountains. We stayed at the fabulous Hong Kong Hotel, which is located on the Kowloon side of the harbor, adjacent to the largest shopping mall in Kowloon. Our hotel room was large, with a beautiful view of the harbor and both a radio and a TV. There were even three English channels, and for $2.00, you could order a movie. The hotel service was excellent. When I pushed the service button in our room, an employee was at our door in 30 seconds. On a morning tour, we saw the Tiger Balm Palace and Garden with its seven-story pagoda; the Cricket Club; St. John's Cathedral; and the Peak Tramway Terminus, from which we traveled by cable car to Victoria Peak for a breathtaking view of the city and harbor. We also visited the beautiful Repulse Bay along the South China Sea and took a ferry ride to see the lights on both sides of Victoria Harbor. Much of our six-day visit was spent shopping, and both Edna and I came home with custom-made clothes.

Honolulu, Hawaii

On the last leg of our journey, we took a flight from Hong Kong to Guam, then on to Hawaii. During the flight, we had lunch, dinner, and breakfast and watched two movies. By this time, we were exhausted and sorely missed the night of sleep we lost as we flew. We left Hong Kong on Saturday evening and arrived in Honolulu 12 hours later— on Saturday morning! A lovely Hawaiian girl welcomed us at the airport with floral leis, and we were then taken to the Ala Moana Hotel on Waikiki Beach. Our room was large and comfortable, with a balcony overlooking Waikiki Beach. The hotel also had a coin-operated laundry, which came in handy at that point in our trip.

Our sightseeing tour in Honolulu included a visit to the University of Hawaii, Mt. Tantalus, and the Punchbowl Crater (a cemetery constructed in the center of an inactive volcano that offered a beautiful view of the city and Diamond Head); a drive along Waikiki Beach; a stop at city hall, and to see the statue of King Kamehameha. Edna and I attended a show at a nightclub that featured various South Pacific dancers, fire dancing and fire eating, and of course, the famous hula dancers. Honolulu offered a combination of beautiful beaches and a South Pacific atmosphere, along with the hustle and bustle of a large metropolitan city. On the flight home, Edna and I reflected on our adventures and all we had learned about Asian cultures.

WEST AFRICA

Edna and I had always wanted to visit Africa, the homeland of our ancestors, and in 1975, we found a tour that included flights, hotels, transfers, food, and sightseeing. The tour took us to five countries: Liberia, Ivory Coast, Nigeria, Ghana, and Togo. Our trip began with a flight on Air Afrique from Washington to Monrovia, Liberia, with stops in New York and Dakar, Senegal. Interestingly, this airline was associated with Air France and owned jointly by 12 West African nations.

Monrovia, Liberia

When we left Washington in December, the temperature was 25 degrees, and when we arrived in Monrovia the next morning, it was 80 degrees. The country of Liberia is the only African nation that has experienced American influences. It was founded by freed slaves from the United States in 1822 and has patterned its government after ours. The city of Monrovia (named after U.S. President James Monroe) was like a country town, with a few 12-story buildings in the downtown area. Most of the people were friendly and spoke English, which is Liberia's official language. Edna and I stayed at the Ducor International Hotel, located on the top of a hill with a picturesque view of the ocean and the city.

Our sightseeing tour of Monrovia began with a drive down Broad Street, the city's main street with tall, modern buildings. We also toured Ashman Street, named after an official of the American Colonization Society who played an important role in the founding of Liberia. Along this street, we saw the Department of State and the Department of Justice. We visited the elegant Presidential Palace, which featured several beautiful flower gardens. The tour concluded with a drive out to the Firestone Rubber Plantation, located 25 miles from Monrovia. On the way, we stopped at a few local markets to buy some fruits.

During our stay in Monrovia, we visited an African woman, Mary Marshall, whom a classmate of Edna's had put us in touch with. Mary and her family prepared a Liberian dinner for us that included peanut butter stew, ham, jollof rice, and Liberian pudding. The Marshalls treated us just as if we were a part of the family, and our visit with them was one of the highlights of our trip.

Abidjan, Ivory Coast

From Monrovia, we flew on Ghana Airlines to Abidjan, the capital of the Ivory Coast. One thing Edna and I quickly learned was that the air travel in Africa was rarely on time, except for international flights. A tour representative who transferred us to our hotel met our tour group at the airport. We stayed at the Ivoire Intercontinental Hotel, which was excellent. Our room was on the 15th floor, with a great view of the city. The hotel facilities included a movie theater, casino, five restaurants, two swimming pools, tennis courts, a bowling alley, golfing, a shopping arcade, and surprisingly, an indoor ice-skating rink. We almost could have spent our entire trip at the hotel!

Our group was given a full day of sightseeing, starting with a visit to the Cocody residential district, featuring luxurious villas, gardens, and a view of the lagoon. We then continued to the colorful Adjame market, where we brought a wood carving and wooden masks. We also visited the IFAN museum, which contains some 25,000 artifacts depicting the history and development of the Ivory Coast. We then drove across the Houphouet-Boigny Bridge to the hub of the city. Our final stop of the morning tour was Treichville Market, a colorful, two-story marketplace, where loincloths and pottery were offered for sale.

In the afternoon, we started with a short tour of Banco Tropical Forest, where Edna fed peanuts to a few wild monkeys. Then, we visited Abidjan University on the way to Dahlia Fleurs, one of the world's most beautiful orchid plantations. We continued to Bingerville for a visit to the African Art School, where we saw beautiful wood carvings made by the students. Our afternoon tour concluded with a visit to a village of the African Ebrie tribe. It was interesting to see the villagers still living in traditional grass huts and mud houses. Abidjan was a well-developed city that offered lots of activities for tourists, but Edna and I also found it to be expensive.

Lagos, Nigeria

After leaving the beautiful city of Abidjan, we arrived in Lagos, Nigeria, where unfortunately, we encountered a number of problems during our three-day visit. Because our airplane was late, we arrived at 11:00 p.m., and the tour group representative took our tired band of travelers to the wrong hotel. Instead of the Ikoyi Hotel in the downtown area, we were driven to the Sphinx Hotel, about 20 miles outside the city. The Sphinx had only two rooms available, and the owners expected part of the group to stay at their private home. The group promptly refused those accommodations and drove back downtown to the Ikoyi Hotel. But the manager there refused to accept our tour vouchers or credit cards, demanding instead payment for two nights in advance and in cash. Our tour leader finally paid the deposit, and although Edna rated the hotel about a C, I was glad to have a room, because I had seen hundreds of people sleeping on the street as we drove through the city. The hotel was located about a mile and a half from downtown with no attractions within walking distance. Edna and I took a taxi to the downtown area at a cost of about $10.00. At the time, the fare was expensive, and the auto traffic in the downtown area was among the worst we had seen. Sitting in a traffic jam for hours was a common occurrence in Lagos.

We were given a morning sightseeing tour of Lagos that included stops at the national museum, which had a fine collection of African art; the national hall and its famous carved Iroko doors, depicting aspects of Nigerian history and culture; the home of the tribal king (Yoruba); and the Independence Building, the tallest building in Nigeria, and its exhibition of Nigerian products.

On our last day in Lagos, Edna and I, along with another couple, hired a chauffeur to drive us around the city. Because the traffic is somewhat lighter on the weekends, the driver agreed to a more reasonable price. Our three-hour private tour took us through the downtown area, along the harbor, out to the beach area, and to the site of the 1977 art and cultural festival.

Accra, Ghana

After leaving Lagos, we traveled to the city of Accra. Edna and I were impressed with the cleanliness of the city and the pride of its residents. We were transferred from the airport to the Ambassador Hotel, where we stayed in a room with both a large ceiling fan and air-conditioning. The room reminded us of a scene in a Humphrey Bogart movie. The hotel was on the beach and had a casino. We were served two meals a day as part of the tour. I really enjoyed the ice cream, which tasted like it was homemade.

We were given a full day of sightseeing in Accra. Our morning tour began with a drive along Liberation Avenue to the campus of the Ghanian Armed Forces. From there, we proceeded to the International Trade Fair site, the Labadi fishing spot, and along Ring Road east to the State House. The tour included the OSU Castle; the Independence Memorial Arch; Independence Square, where official ceremonies are held; the American Embassy; Parliament House; the National Museum; the Trade Union Congress Hall; and the downtown market. For lunch, the tour driver took us to the Ebony Restaurant, where we enjoyed some local specialties.

In the afternoon, we drove through Liberty Avenue to Achimota School, where most of Ghana's early educators studied. Our visit to the University of Ghana featured many lovely tropical gardens for us to stroll through. The tour continued into the mountains, where we visited some native villages, and concluded with a visit to a century-old botanical garden. There, we sampled the fruit of trees from various parts of Africa and India. Edna and I enjoyed Accra more than any other city we visited during our tour of West Africa. The city's symbol was the Black Star, which was visible on most of the buildings. Most of the people spoke English and were very friendly, and we were gratified to see a city where Blacks operated most of the businesses.

Lome, Togo

We traveled by van from Accra about two hours along a coastal road to Lome, Togo. In Lome, we stayed in a small but comfortable room on the ocean at the Le Benin Hotel. We arrived on Christmas Eve, and because many West Africans celebrate Christmas as we do in America, the hotel had a large Christmas tree in the lobby. In the afternoon, we strolled through the small town and visited the market. While we were shopping, we met Parfait, a young man who offered to carry our shopping bags. Parfait was a native of Togo and spoke both French and English. We were happy to pay him a few dollars a day to show us around town and serve as our French translator.

Edna and I had delicious meals in the hotel and, for entertainment, visited a couple of swinging nightclubs. Togo was our last stop on the trip and a good place to relax. On Christmas Day, we took a morning sightseeing tour of Lome, driving by the Presidential Palace and Independence Square, with its monuments. We also visited the History Museum of Kponton. In the afternoon, we relaxed on the beach, enjoying the crystal-clear water and calm waves. Our stay in Lome was wonderful way to spend Christmas Day and conclude an enjoyable and educational trip to West Africa.

CRUISE FROM SAN JUAN TO SOUTH AMERICA

For our next trip, Edna and I planned to take our first cruise. In August 1976, we flew to San Juan, Puerto Rico, to board the *Carla C* to South America, with stops in Curacao, Caracas, Trinidad, Martinique, and St. Thomas. We arrived in San Juan four days before the cruise so that we could enjoy the attractions of the city, including the historical sights in old San Juan, the high-rise development and shopping district, nightclub shows and gambling, and the opportunity to swim on the beautiful beaches.

The *Carla C* was like a floating wonderland with plenty of activities: two swimming pools, a movie theater with different movies each day, two large ballrooms that featured music and live entertainment nightly, a casino, a card room, musical horse races, and bingo. Dining on the ship was elegant. We were served breakfast, lunch, dinner, and a midnight buffet and enjoyed such dishes as prime rib, filet mignon, lobster, and duck in orange sauce. On the downside, our inside stateroom on the *Carla C* offered barely enough room to move around in, and Edna was seasick for most of the trip, unable to get used to the rocking of the ship.

Throughout the trip, we stopped at a number of interesting ports for sightseeing and shopping. We spent one day in each port and sailed during the night. Our first stop was Curacao in the Netherlands Antilles.

Curacao

The capital city of Curacao, Willemstad, offered a bit of the old Holland atmosphere in the Caribbean. The residents of Curacao spoke three languages, Papiamento (a native form of Dutch), Dutch, and English. In port, we had a sightseeing tour that covered the Autonomy Monument, built to symbolize the unity of the six islands of the Netherlands Antilles; the Franklin D. Roosevelt House, the residence and office of the U.S. Consul General; the old residential sections of Scharloo; Mikve Israel, the oldest synagogue in the Western Hemisphere, built in 1732; the mansion Chobolobo; and a Jewish cemetery, the oldest Caucasian burial ground in the Americas, dating back to 1650. Our tour concluded with a stop at the beautiful Curacao Hilton Hotel.

Caracas

Our ship next docked at the seaport of La Guaira, about 20 miles from the city of Caracas. We hired a taxi driver to take us around to the sights. Since Edna and I had visited Caracas about two years earlier, we knew the best attractions to visit. Our driver, Louis, spoke very good English and showed us a wonderful time. Caracas, the capital of Venezuela, is a scenic city with both high-rise developments and breathtaking mountains that surround the city. Our tour included the Simon Bolivar Center, the country club section, the famous Officers Club, and a stop at the Tamanaco Hotel. We had lunch at a local restaurant and later stopped at a juice stand for refreshments. On the way back to the ship, we stopped at the Macuto Sheraton, located on a lovely portion of the beach and where Edna and I had stayed on our previous visit to Venezuela.

Trinidad

In Trinidad, Daisy Aleong, the cousin of my friend Al Ottley, met us at the ship and took us under her wing for a fun-filled day. Her tour of the capital city, Port of Spain, included the Government House, the botanical gardens, Trinidad's War Memorial, Queen's Royal College, the country club section, and a drive through the exclusive Maraval residential district. We had lunch at a new Holiday Inn and, later that afternoon, stopped by Daisy's house for some homemade punch and passion fruit juice. Our visit to Trinidad was quite enjoyable but too short; the ship had arrived at noon, and we had to be back onboard by 6:00.

Martinique

The island of Martinique adds a touch of French flavor to the spice of the West Indies. Martinique's close ties with France since the 17th century have given the island a unique charm, resulting from the harmonious blend of French and West Indian traditions. The island is the birthplace of Napoleon's wife, Empress Josephine. Our ship dropped anchor about a mile out in the harbor, and we were transported to shore by motorboats. The harbor was located in the heart of Fort-de-France, the capital and largest city on Martinique. We browsed the downtown shops and markets before returning to the ship. In the afternoon, we were entertained onboard ship by a Martinique cultural dance group.

St. Thomas

Our ship arrived in St. Thomas in the U.S. Virgin Islands about 10:00 in the morning. From the ship, we had a picturesque view of Charlotte Amalie's harbor. Charlotte Amalie offers the typical atmosphere of a Caribbean town, with winding streets, delightful shops, and continental flavor. The city was built along a steep mountain, and the water in the harbor is a majestic light blue. We took a taxicab ride up the mountain road to Bluebeard's Castle, the hideout of the famous pirate. From the castle, we had a panoramic view of Charlotte Amalie and its harbor. Edna and I particularly enjoyed shopping in St. Thomas, where the shops were tidy and the prices, reasonable.

Our cruise on the *Carla C* ended when we arrived back in San Juan. Although the cruise was enjoyable and the accommodations were luxurious, Edna had had enough of the ship's rocking and wasn't excited about the idea of taking another cruise anytime soon. For my part, I found the experience on this "floating hotel" quite enjoyable, and I was delighted to see so many islands in a short period of time.

MONTREAL, CANADA

In October 1976, Edna and I flew to Montreal, second only to Paris as the largest French-speaking city in the world. The city is an island, surrounded by both the St. Lawrence and Ottawa rivers, but Montreal has overcome its island confinement by growing skyward. Forty-story buildings have replaced many of the ancient structures; however, the charm of the 18th- and 19th-century buildings has been preserved in an old city section. The old city of Montreal provided a vivid contrast to its 20th-century architecture. On a leisurely walking tour of old Montreal, Edna and I saw Notre–Dame Basilica, with its neo-Gothic design and magnificent carved-wood altar; the nearby Maisonneuve Monument, named for Paul Chomedey de Maisonneuve, who laid the foundation of Montreal's first home in 1642; Place Royale, the city's oldest landmark, dating back to 1676; the Montreal Courthouse; Place Jacques-Cartier, formerly an outdoor marketplace where various artworks are displayed; Bonsecours Market, the city hall prior to 1879; Notre-Dame de Bonsecour, dating back to 1771; and the City Hall building.

Edna and I also spent a good bit of time riding the efficient and convenient Montreal subway system. Each station is designed with its own unique character. Downtown, the subway connected with an underground system of shopping malls. We rode the subway to the island in the St. Lawrence River where the 1967 exposition entitled Man and His World was held. On the island was an aquarium, holding numerous tropical fish, penguins, and a large shark. The subway was also convenient for visiting the Olympic Village and Stadium. From the subway, we took a walking tour of the Olympic site.

At the time we were in Montreal, the city had about 60,000 Black residents, the majority of them immigrants from the West Indies. We visited a Black nightclub, Rockhead's Paradise, with a downstairs bar that featured a jazz combo and a live rhythm-and-blues show upstairs. The club's atmosphere was popping, the entertainers were very good, and we really partied. Our evening at Rockhead's may well have been the highlight of our four-day visit to Montreal.

Chapter 4

STARTING MY OWN BUSINESS

—〜〜—

In the fall of 1977, Edna and I purchased a two-bedroom condo in Falls Church, VA. Our condo is on the 12th floor and has a beautiful view of Washington, DC, including the Capitol and the Washington Monument. On the 4th of July, we love to sit on our balcony and watch the fireworks as they shoot up over these landmarks.

By 1977, I had completed the booklet about my family and my book about our travels around the world. I was looking for a new project. I was a senior-level employee with the Council of Governments, and Edna was a head nurse at Doctor's Hospital in DC. We had wanted to have some children but couldn't. I knew that starting a business would give us a back-up income. I thought about starting a transportation planning consulting company, but I didn't have the money or the contacts.

A friend and previous co-worker, Bob Cosby, told me about a business he was starting. He knew we liked to take trips, and he said that we could do business while traveling. He invited me to a business meeting at his home. Edna didn't want to attend, but she told me to get the information and keep her posted. Bob told me that business attire was expected at the meeting, which was fine with me because I wore a tie to work every day. Before I left for the meeting, Bob called and asked me to bring some folding chairs. About that time, Edna got curious and decided to go with me. We had been to a few vacation condo sales presentations, and Edna thought she'd better come along to make sure I didn't spend any money.

Bob and his wife, Sherion, welcomed us into their home, and the meeting began. The Cosbys' upline, John Crowe, showed the business plan. John was just 27 years old and had just achieved financial freedom. Neither Edna nor I had ever heard of Amway, but with John's talk of financial freedom and travel, he got our interest.

At the meeting, we also met the Cosbys' sponsors, Glenn and Lynda Young. We were fortunate to have great mentors like Glenn and Lynda, as well as John and Jenniebelle Crowe. On the way home in the car, I told Edna that we should join. The worst thing we could do is to purchase the products at Independent Business Owner (IBO) cost. I didn't believe that I could become financially free, but I did think I could make an extra $10,000 a year. I liked the idea of being a business owner versus getting a part-time job.

Because the product line was mostly cleaning products, our first step was to try the products, and we liked them, so we knew we could sell them. Back then, showing the business plan took two to three hours, but I was determined to find a shortcut. I created standard and large flipcharts without asking my upline, mostly because I was used to doing presentations at work with flipcharts. I was criticized for creating the flipcharts because my downline would be unable to duplicate them. I finally purchased a white board and learned the business plan by using index cards. Of course, years later, we started using a hand-size flipchart presentation. Today, the business plan is on a DVD and online and requires less than 10 minutes to view.

At first, our business didn't move very fast, because we were not fully committed to it. We used the products, and I showed the business plan about one or two times a week. It was not until a few months later, when Edna and I attended a major function, Free Enterprise Day (FED), that we became committed to the business.

FED weekend was held at the coliseum in Greensboro, NC. There, we saw George and Ruth Halsey being honored as the first Black Diamonds in Amway. George and Ruth said, if we can do it, then you can, too. They motivated us to set a goal to go Diamond. We also saw Dexter and Birdie Yager and Bill and Peggy Britt, and Dexter gave me one of my mottos: If the dream is big enough, then the facts don't count—just do it! Bill Britt convinced me that whatever we say can come true. If you think you can and will say it, it will happen, which also means that you should say only what you want to become reality.

Driving home after that weekend, Edna and I set a goal to become financially independent. The business plan was to go Diamond in two to five years and make $150,000 per year. I figured that I could do anything hard for one year. I was willing to commit 12 months to showing the business plan six or seven nights a week in order to be financially free. I was 30 years old at the time, and I could picture myself being financially free with no job in one year. I had heard a motivational tape by Bob Harrington, who said, "It is fun making money," so I decided to make that saying my slogan. I was going to work my business and make it fun. I believed that everyone could be successful by doing something they enjoyed. My goal was to show the business plan to everyone I liked and let them decide whether or not to join. I wouldn't try to convince anyone; I would just make the offer. We call this approach SW, SW, SW: Some will, some won't, and so what? For those who are not looking to make some extra money, then give them a sample product and make them a customer. I just wanted everyone to know about my business and the fact that they had a chance to join. In turn, I wanted to find out what their dreams were. I figured out to stop offering steak to vegetarians; offer them some vegetables instead.

I learned how to use the Britt World Wide (BWW) training system. BWW provides training tapes (now CDs), books, and seminars. I found out that people who listened to tapes, read books that promoted a positive mental attitude, and attended seminars would stay positive about the business. In that year, I presented 30 to 35 business plans per month. Edna and I didn't reach our goal of financial freedom in a year, but we made $3,000 a month as Platinum IBOs. We reset our goal to be financially free in 12 months. At the end of the next year, I started saving my regular salary as a civil engineer. That is one of the best feelings you will ever experience: to get your check at work and not need the money. I kept working because I enjoyed my profession and had a good boss. Working shifts was stressful for Edna, so she decided to leave her job and stay home.

Some people will tell you that the business won't work and you can't do it. One of my co-workers had that negative attitude. We used to go to the bank together every other Friday. When the payroll checks got to our floor we knew, because they were delivered from a squeaky rolling cart. When we heard, "squeak, squeak, squeak," we knew it was time to stop work and go to the bank. Back then, I was a "smart engineer"; I mailed my bills on Thursday before payday, which meant I had to deposit my check on Friday to cover the bills. One day, two years after setting my goal to be financially free, we heard the paychecks coming, and my co-worker said, "Are you going to the bank?" I smiled and replied, "My Amway business is going so good that I don't have to go to the bank." That day was the first time I could hold my civil engineering paycheck as extra income.

Another two weeks went by before we heard the "squeak, squeak, squeak" of the pay cart. Again, my co-worker asked me if I was going to the bank, and I said no and showed him my check from two weeks ago. The look on his face was priceless. I set up a savings account and banked all of my engineering salary for a year. I would get a check, put it in my wallet, and carry it around for two weeks. Then, on the Thursday before payday, I would deposit it into my savings account because I would get a new check to carry around the next day.

At this point, Edna and I were at the Emerald level in Amway and were helping three IBOships to the Platinum level. Our Platinum IBOs were Ray Hammiel, Horace Harris, and Darryl and Miriam Norton. I was wondering if I should quit my job and felt the need to counsel with my mentor. Edna and I went to spend the day with our upline mentors, Bill and Peggy Britt, in Chapel Hill, NC. That trip changed my life. Bill and Peggy owned an estate with two beautiful homes on it. Edna spent time with Peggy in her garden, and I had fun with Bill, looking at his fancy cars. I remember sitting in his Rolls Royce, and he said, "G.W., you can have a Rolls Royce, too." I asked Bill whether I should quit my job, and he asked me if I hated it. I said no, but I just didn't want to keep going into the office. Bill looked at my business organization and advised me to keep working until I hit the Diamond level in Amway, which means helping six IBOships to the Platinum level. He said, "You are close to it now; just keep showing the business plan at the same rate."

Then Bill continued: "When you go Diamond, we will have a very special freedom banquet in your honor. We will use the Washington Hilton ballroom and have more than 2,000 people come to celebrate your financial freedom. It will be a black-tie affair, and we will have a Rolls Royce to pick up you and your family. It will be an event that the people in Washington, DC, will never forget."

With those words, Bill built my dream. Edna and I left Bill and Peggy's home with a commitment to get Diamond accomplished. Like Bill said, I just kept showing the business plan. A year later, Edna and I were qualified Diamond and the dream came true. Our freedom banquet was at the Washington Hilton ballroom on August 20, 1981, with more than 2,000 people in attendance. The event was phenomenal. I only regret that my father had passed away two years earlier and could not see what I had accomplished. It was great to have my mother and Edna's mother sitting at the head table with us, along with my personal Platinums and Bill and Peggy Britt. My mother said that she had never shaken so many hands in her life! Horace Harris (who was Emerald at the time and went on to be our first Diamond) was the master of ceremonies. We were presented with numerous awards, and our six Platinum legs all spoke. The speakers were Ray Hammiel, Horace Harris, Darryl and Miriam Norton, Tony Gainor, Myrtle Louise Burford and Evelyn Anderson (my cousins who are sisters and a partnership in business), and my sister Nana Robinson. Bill and Peggy Britt also gave a speech, which was the highlight of the night. What a dream banquet! Washington Hilton waiters marched in the dessert (flaming baked Alaska) as the lights dimmed in the ballroom and marching music played. After three and a half years, it was truly a dream come true.

The next day, we flew to Bermuda for a seminar with all the Britt Diamonds. Try to imagine how I felt: I was 33 years old and financially free. I had said goodbye to filling out leave slips, waking up to an alarm clock, listening to a boss tell me how long I had to stay at work, and fighting rush-hour traffic. It was great to be with the Britt Diamonds in Bermuda, where we stayed at the South Hampton Princess Hotel. It was also good just to relax, because for two years, we had being paying the price for financial freedom by showing the business plan six to seven nights per week.

Of course, because I always listened to Bill, I was on the beach in a long-sleeved dress shirt. Bill had advised me that if I wanted to be successful, then I had to look successful by wearing a dark suit; a white, long-sleeved shirt; and a tie with some red in it. "Look like you are on Wall Street," Bill said. Two years earlier, I had given all my regular shirts to Goodwill and purchased all long–sleeved, white shirts from my own business. When you join Amway and become an IBO, you get a name for your business. Our business is King International, and we are proud to purchase from ourselves. Amway stands for the American Way, and the company offers people a way to have their own independent businesses. In 1959, Rich DeVos and Jay Van Andel started Amway with cleaning products. When I started my business, Amway had just launched the Personal Shoppers Catalog, which offers clothes, gifts, and toys, so I was able to purchase my white shirts from the catalog. I did, however, finally break down and purchase some casual shirts for the beach. Amway is now run by the founders' sons, Doug DeVos and Steve Van Andel, and its major product focus is health and beauty. The company also has a number of partner stores, such as Sears, K-Mart, Best Buy,

Office Depot, Bass Pro Shops, and Dick's Sporting Goods. In 2010, Amway had worldwide sales of $9.2 billion.

One of the most memorable events during the trip occurred while a few of the men and I—Bill Britt, Dave Taylor, Paul Miller, Rocky Covington, and Ron Puryear—were just relaxing in the ocean, all holding onto a raft. I asked Bill a question: "What would it take for me to move on to Double Diamond level?" Bill said, "Let me show you," and he promptly pushed my head under water. I wasn't worried at first, because I knew that Bill wouldn't hurt me, but after several seconds, I grew short of air and struggled to come up. I sputtered to Bill, "Don't kill me on my first day of freedom!" Bill asked, "G.W., when you were under the water, what was the most important thing you wanted?" "A breath of air," I replied, and Bill said, "When you want Double Diamond as bad as you wanted that breath of air, you will have it."

The biggest thrill in going Diamond was being honored at the FED weekend and having Bill and Peggy hold up our hands as the theme from *Rocky* played. More than 10,000 excited IBOs cheered us on.

In January, Amway sent us to the Diamond Club in Hawaii, and in the spring, the company sent us to Peter Island in the British Virgin Islands, which is owned by Amway. It was funny to me to realize that once we had plenty of money and could afford really nice trips, then we traveled for free. Amway certainly knows how to make its IBOs feel important on these all-expense-paid trips.

We took one trip to Peter Island with Angelo and Claudia Nardone, a couple who had gone Diamond at the same time that we did. Angelo asked me to go sailing with him, and I agreed, but I told him that I wasn't a great swimmer and didn't want to go too far out in the water. Angelo said, "No problem. We'll just go and have a little fun." I put on a life jacket as we got into the two-passenger sailboat and sat back to enjoy the ride.

Angelo and I could see Edna and Claudia on the beach, but the longer we sailed, the smaller they got. After about an hour, I told Angelo that I thought we should go back to shore. That's when he told me he had been trying to go back for about 20 minutes. I panicked and asked what I could do to help. We just could not get the boat to go in the right direction. We tried so hard that we turned the boat over. There we were out in the Caribbean Sea, with the boat upside down and paddling with our hands. Finally, a motorboat came by and pulled us to shore. We were able to laugh at ourselves, but it was good to be back on dry land. I had gripped the boat so hard that my fingerprints were still on the hull. When we got back home, Edna and I enrolled in a swimming class. A few years later, we took our second trip to Peter Island on my birthday. This time, we went with Diamonds Hal and Esther Newball and our upline Double Diamonds John and Jenniebelle Crowe. It was another great trip, and although I didn't go sailing, I did go back to see if my fingerprints were still on that sailboat.

Chapter 5

DREAMS COME TRUE

—◦◦◦—

When we started our business, Edna and I wrote down a list of dreams and put them on the refrigerator. Our big dream was to become financially independent and not have to work a job. We wanted to be able to pay off all our bills and not have money control us. Of course, you will always have to pay taxes and insurance, but the dream of not having a home mortgage, a car note, and revolving credit-card debt was high on our list, and we accomplished it. One of the books I used to get out of debt was *Rapid Debt Reduction Strategies* by John Avanzini with Patrick Ondrey.

One of the keys to accomplishing your dreams is to first write them down and date them; then develop a plan and work the plan. Find someone who has done what you are trying to accomplish and listen to that person. Proverbs 27:17 tells us: "Iron sharpeneth iron; so a man sharpeneth the countenance of his friend." I counsel with Bill Britt, who is now Founders Crown Ambassador in Amway in the United States and Crown in India. Below are listed some of the dreams Edna and I were able to accomplish by listening to Bill and working toward that list on our refrigerator.

1) A trip to Rio de Janeiro when we went Platinum in the

business. We left the cold of Washington, DC, in February, and when we arrived in Rio, the temperature was 80 degrees.

2) A new Mercedes Benz for Edna when we helped our first Platinum, which was Ray Hammiel.

3) A week's vacation every month for the past 30 years. One of our dreams was to relax and have fun. Edna and I work our business as we travel, but we also know how to have fun. I like staying in the best hotels and eating the best food. Edna likes salmon, and my favorite food is chicken. I travel all around the world looking for the best chicken.

4) Ownership of a Rolls Royce. When we visited Bill and Peggy Britt before we achieved Diamond, I had sat in Bill's Rolls Royce, and he told me, "One day, you will have one." Then, in December 1981, he told me it was time to get my Rolls. We had our new Rolls Royce Silver Shadow II delivered at the Winter Conference in Washington, DC. The salesman drove the Rolls into the Wardman Park Marriott exhibition hall while thousands of people sat at their tables having dinner. Later that night, I surprised Edna on stage with a full-length black ranch mink coat. I'm not sure which of us was more excited that night!

5) Ownership of an Excalibur. I had a picture of this fancy automobile with tires on the side, running boards, and a big front grill on my refrigerator for two years. In 1982, Edna and I had an Excalibur custom built for us. The Excalibur cost $75,000, which I had in my bank account, but instead of writing the dealer a check, I charged the car on my American Express card. That way, I earned points for airline tickets when I wrote the check to American Express.

6) A new Mercedes Benz 300D for my mother. The keys were presented to her on stage at the Winter Conference at the Hyatt Regency in Baltimore. My mother and my sister Jean had supported us in our Amway business. They built their business and became our seventh Platinum leg. As it turned out, buying the Benz for my mother was a good investment. It still runs fine, and we use it when we travel to the St. Louis area. The Benz has also been truly a family car. It was passed down to Jean after my mother died and to Jean's daughter, Andrea Callahan, after Jean died. Andrea also now has Mother and Jean's Amway business.

7) A trip for my mother and both sisters, Nana and Jean, to London and Paris. This trip remains one of my best memories. Nana wanted to see the Big Ben Clock Tower in London, and Jean was always talking about seeing the Eiffel Tower in Paris. Edna and I took them on what I called the limo tour: Every time we walked out of the hotel, there was a limo waiting to drive us around.

8) The opportunity to watch my mother and sisters achieve their dreams. My mother and both sisters were able to retire early from their jobs. Jean purchased her dream car, a Jaguar, and built a home in Orlando with a swimming pool and Jacuzzi. Nana lived in the home all year, and mother and Jean came down to stay in the winter. Every Christmas, Edna and I visited Orlando, and other family members came from East St. Louis and Cleveland for a big dinner on Christmas Day. Dennis would drive Andrea, Darian, Jessica, and Arielle down from East St. Louis, and Darrell, Vivian, and Royce would fly in from Cleveland. Also joining us were Robert and Ardell Bush and their family

and Raymond, Doris, Daris, and Hunter Cason. We had fun going to Disney World, Universal Studios, and Sea World and visiting with Diamonds Rick and Toni Fairchild.

9) An annual trip to Las Vegas for Edna's mother. Mama Adams could get around with a walker, but I always ordered a motor chair for her to drive around the casinos and play the slots. Edna and I don't gamble, but we loved watching Mama Adams having fun. I spent most of my time in Vegas in the game room playing video games. We also enjoyed going to shows to hear such singers as Gladys Knight, the Temptations, and the Four Tops. One night, as we sat close to the stage, the Four Tops sang to Mama. The look on her face was priceless! We also met Neil Taffe, one of the back-up singers in Gladys Knight's show. Now, Edna and I look forward to having lunch with Neil on our visits to Las Vegas. On our last trip, we were able spend some time with our downline Effie Young, who lives in Las Vegas.

10) The chance to spend special time with Rich DeVos, the President of Amway at the time of our meeting. Because Edna is an alumnus of Howard University, Amway invited us to a fundraiser lunch at which the company donated $10,000 to Howard's scholarship fund. President Ronald Reagan was the guest speaker for the luncheon. We sat at the table with Rich DeVos and the Prime Minister of the British Virgin Islands (where Amway owns Peter Island). We were surprised when our table was invited to come backstage to personally meet President Reagan and First Lady Nancy Reagan. Of course, the President asked to take a picture with us. WOW! That afternoon truly was a dream come true.

Chapter 6

BUILDING OUR BUSINESS AROUND THE WORLD

—✺—

Edna and I were fortunate that in the early 1990s, Amway launched a number of global markets. Because we were financially free and liked to travel, we attended many of the global market launches. Britt World Wide (BWW) empowers men and women to build successful independent businesses by providing education and mentorship to an association of business leaders across North America and the world. The BWW Management Operating Committee consists of Bill and Peggy Britt, Paul and Leslie Miller, Kanti and Lata Gala, Angelo and Claudia Nardone, Shivaram and Anjali Kumar, and Raj and Sangita Shah. This chapter offers an overview of the countries Edna and I traveled to, and the people who traveled with us and hosted us.

THE AMERICAS

Argentina

Amway launched the market for Argentina in March

1993. Edna and I traveled to Buenos Aires and stayed at the Plaza Hotel. Our friend Marcus Von Goihman, who lives in our condo complex, met us in Buenos Aires. Marcus is from Argentina and served as our interpreter. Our contact person in Buenos Aires was Julio Blanco, referred to us by George and Barbara Queen. We returned to Buenos Aires in November 1993 with Claude and Janice Allen, downline in Bishop Lewis and Ann Tait's organization in the United States. Because Claude spoke Spanish, he interpreted for my home meetings. We stayed at the Marriott Plaza Hotel, along with some of the bodyguards for Michael Jackson, who was doing a show at the stadium. We made friends with the guards, and they gave us free VIP tickets to the show. Afterwards, we went backstage and rode on the bus with the musicians. It was an exciting show.

Barbados

In Barbados, we stayed on the beach at the Marriott Sam Lords Castle. How nice it was to show the business plan with the Caribbean Sea in the background. When I reflect on Barbados, I think of Wayne Callender, who was born in Barbados. Edna and I are proud of Wayne and his wife, Suzanne, who are Executive Diamonds on the BWW Team.

Brazil

Edna and I were invited by BWW to be the guest speakers at a seminar in San Paulo, Brazil, in December 1996 at the Intercontinental Hotel. Our hosts, Marco and Helena Pinho, met us at the airport after listening to our rally story cassette tape in the car.

Canada

During March 1995, Edna and I did Diamond open meetings, showing the business plan, in Saskatoon and Calgary. In June 1996, we did a Diamond open meeting in Montreal, where we had a delightful time with André and Françoise Blanchard. In May 2002, we were the guest speakers for a seminar in Calgary at the Hyatt Regency. Our host couple was Gary and Linda Sadden, who also drove us to Banff for a day tour.

Chile

Amway launched the opening of the market in Chile in February 1995. Edna and I flew to Santiago and stayed at the Hyatt Regency. Our downline IBOs Steve and Kym Taylor, who live in Lanham, MD, met us in Santiago. We showed a number of business plans during our visit but took time to watch the Superbowl with Steve and Kym at our hotel.

Costa Rico

We were invited by BWW to be the guest speakers at a seminar in San Jose in April 1996. Our host, Francisco Diana, met us at the airport and took us to a nearby Marriott. We enjoyed spending time with Russell Youngblood, the son of Diamonds Ray and Carroll Youngblood.

El Salvador

Amway launched the opening of the market in El Salvador in January 1995. Edna and I traveled to San

Salvador for the market launch. We were also invited back by BWW to be guest speakers at a seminar there in April 1996.

Guatemala

We were invited by BWW to be the guest speakers at a seminar in Guatemala City in April 1996. Our host couple was Rudy and Zoila Juarez. Their son Chachi took us sightseeing to the town of Antigua, where the jade factories are located. Yes, I bought a lot of jade that day for Edna.

Honduras

We were in Tegucigalpa for an Amway launch in January 1995, and in April 1996, we were the guest speakers for seminars in Tegucigalpa and San Pedro Sula. On this trip, we first spoke in Guatemala City, and then our hosts, Rudy and Ziola again, traveled with us to Honduras. Doris Dacarett de Santos was the interpreter for Edna in San Pedro Sula. She is the upline for our team in Honduras and sponsors our leaders, Russell and Paulette Hogan, in the Honduras market. Russell and Paulette are downline in Richard and Carolyn Mosby's organization in the United States.

Mexico

In April 1993, we did a seminar for the BWW Team in Mexico City. Our hosts in Mexico City were Ricardo and Debbie Gonzales, friends of ours who used to live in the Washington, DC, area. They showed us a great time. In October 1997 and again in November 2002, we were invited by BWW to speak in Monterrey. During the 2002 trip, we also did a seminar in Guadalajara. In Monterrey, the Britt leaders were Oscar and Diane Harper, and our hosts were Benito and Lourdes Bonilla. In Guadalajara, Enrique and Claudia Camacho Felix hosted us.

Uruguay

We traveled to Montevideo for the Amway market launch in November 1995. One of the highlights of this trip was spending special time at the opening reception with Dick DeVos, the son of Amway founder Rich DeVos and President of Amway at the time. It was also great to spend time with Quentin and Nena Hardy, the son and daughter-in-law of Diamonds Terral and Margaret Hardy.

EUROPE

Belgium

In April 1997, Edna and I were invited to speak at the Ron and Toby Hale / Jerry and Sherry Meadows Spring Leadership Conference in Oostende, Belgium. Interestingly, the conference was interpreted in several languages. I also remember staying up late that Sunday night to watch Tiger Woods win his first Masters Tournament on TV.

Czech Republic

We were in Prague in the Czech Republic for the Amway market launch in March 1994, along with our downline Steve and Kym Taylor. The BWW meetings were at the beautiful Atrium Hotel. We were also invited by BWW to be the guest speakers at seminars in Prague and Brno in November 2001, where we were hosted by Michal Grivna.

France

In June 1995, Edna and I traveled to Paris to show the business plan at the open meeting for André and Françoise Blanchard. We were also guest speakers at their leadership conference. During our visit, we went to the Paris Disneyland, mainly because I wanted to see if Mickey spoke English. In May 2000, we took my mother and two sisters, Nana and Jean, to Paris and London. That was our famous limo tour, with chauffeured cars waiting for us every time we walked out of a hotel. Our downline Gilles Fourcault, who lives in Baltimore but was from Paris, met us in the city. Art Jefferson sponsored Gilles in the U.S. business. Gilles showed the business plan in Paris to his cousin Eva Sankate, and he and Eva showed Edna and me a great time in Paris.

Germany

Our German business started when one of our downline, Oudia Prevost, met a German woman, Gisela Petzold, and her husband at the Washington, DC, Hilton. Horace Harris sponsored Oudia, and Oudia, in turn, sponsored the Petzolds internationally; they achieved the Platinum level in Germany in 1980. We have since traveled to Germany several times to show the business plan and have been invited as guest speakers at seminars.

Edna and I set up a number two Amway business in Germany downline from Gisela. In March 1996, we had the opportunity to have lunch with Gisela and one of her downline, a couple who is now Ruby in the Amway German business. One of our most memorable trips was in July 1993, when we traveled by car with Rick and Helen Justis. They were in the military, with assignments in Germany. Their upline in the United States are Diamonds Bobby and Priscilla Harris. Rick and Helen took us from the Frankfurt area down through Bavaria. During the trip, we stopped and had lunch with Ursula, who is the sister of Ingeborg Schleier-Smith, the wife of my cousin Shedd Smith. Ursula had traveled with us by car to the Midwest during her visit to the United States, and it was nice to see her again. We spent one night in a beautiful hotel overlooking Oberammergau, a town known for its passion play. We continued on to Munich, where we showed the business plan at the open meeting. We have also shown the business plan and done seminars in Frankfurt, Kaiserslautern, Ramstein, Furth, Nurnberg, Hofheim, Hamburg, and Ansbach. Tom and Darilyn Shaver, Doug and Carmen Haines, Eddie and Joan Collins, Norm and Josie Daley, and John and Tahanna Rush, among others, have hosted us.

Greece

Edna and I were in Athens for the Amway market launch in March 1996, and in April 1997, we were invited by BWW to be the guest seminar speakers in three locations in Greece. We spoke in Athens, Thessaloniki, and Heraklion, the capital city of the island of Crete. Sophia was our host in Greece.

Italy

We spent our 32nd wedding anniversary in Rome and Venice in September 2003. On the way back from speaking at a leadership conference in Turkey, we decided to celebrate our anniversary in Italy. We spent five wonderful nights in Rome and five in Venice.

Norway

In May 2011, Edna and I flew from Copenhagen, Denmark, to Oslo, Norway, where we were met by Tom Egil Johnsen and his wife, Gry. Our hosts did a great job of making us feel welcome. Tom drove us to his hometown of Tonsberg, about an hour and half from Oslo and the oldest city in Norway. There, we stayed at the Quality Inn in a room with a great view of the water. We did a seminar for the BWW Team members, who were fired up to see us. Ruby IBOs Vidar and Mariann Sonesen also hosted the meeting. The next day, Tom and Gry took us sightseeing. Our trip to Scandinavia was truly enjoyable. The people were very friendly and almost everyone spoke English. We loved sharing the message that "it is fun making money!"

Poland

Edna and I were the guest speakers at a seminar in Warsaw, Poland, in July 1993. We were hosted by Mariola Laskowska and stayed at the Marriott Hotel. Our downline in Warsaw was Anna Bhutani, who was internationally sponsored by Dr. Leo Pickett of Forestville, MD. Mariola and Anna showed us a great time and took us sightseeing during our visit to Warsaw. We also had fun with Mike

Zuhr and Al Bala, who was CEO of BWW at the time. In March and July 1994, we returned to Warsaw to show the business plan at an open meeting, and in November 2001, we were invited to speak at another BWW seminar. In July 2003, we were invited to speak at the Success Conference in Warsaw.

Slovak Republic

We were in Bratislava in the Slovak Republic for the Amway market launch in November 1994, staying at the Hotel Bratislava. In August 1996, we were invited to be the guest speakers for the seminars in Kosice and Presov. In Presov, we stayed at the Atrium Hotel.

Spain

Edna and I visited Madrid, Spain, in August 2011, along with my niece Andrea Callahan (my sister Jean's daughter) and her two daughters, Jessica (age 22) and Arielle (age 13). This was the first trip outside of the United States for them. For us, Spain was the 52nd foreign country that we had visited. We stayed at a lovely Hilton near the airport. My nieces enjoyed the executive lounge, which offered unlimited soft drinks and served food three times a day. We met with some of the BWW leaders, including Hellen, Jill, Celia, and Villamor, who were very excited about the business. In a fine example of duplication, we had lunch at the same restaurant, sitting at the same table, where Bill Britt ate during his visit to Madrid. And if Bill ordered chicken, you know we had the same meal! After lunch, my nieces went to the nearby wax museum; then, we went to see a movie that was in English with Spanish subtitles. My nieces even went to see a bullfight. We have many great memories from that trip.

Sweden

In May 2011, Edna and I flew to Copenhagen, Denmark, which is across the water (the Oresund Strait) from Malmo, the third largest city in Sweden. The leaders for this trip were Platinums Pelle and Maria Lundgren, who made us feel right at home. Pelle meet us at the Copenhagen airport, and we then took the train for the 12-minute ride to Malmo. How convenient that the train station was in the airport. In Malmo, we stayed at the Renaissance Hotel in the historic area near the train station.

Scandinavia is known for its salmon, which is a favorite of Edna's. She had salmon every day, even for breakfast. Of course, my favorite—chicken—was also available. On one day of our visit, we did a seminar for the BWW Team members, who were excited and ready to learn. Pelle and Maria also took us sightseeing and bowling and invited us to dinner with their family.

Turkey

Edna and I traveled to Istanbul, Turkey, for the Amway market launch in July 1994. Our downline Oray and Ayse Esiner met us in Istanbul. The two were from Turkey, but Oray had worked in the Washington, DC, area for TWA with my cousin Bill Anderson. Bill and his wife, Doris, were downline from my cousins Evelyn Anderson and Myrtle Louise Burford. In Istanbul, we stayed at the Hilton Hotel and had a beautiful view of the water from our room. We showed the business plan to numerous people during the launch.

Our second visit to Turkey was also with Oray and Ayse, in November 1994. We showed the business plan at the open meetings in Istanbul, Izmir, and Ankara. We also went sightseeing with Oray and Ayse, took a boat ride in Istanbul, and did a lot of shopping. Some rugs we selected were sent back for us to the United States. When we were in Izmir, we took a day tour of the ancient city of Ephesus.

In February 1996, we traveled back to Turkey and again spoke at the open meetings in Istanbul, Izmir, and Ankara. We were also invited by BWW to be the guest speakers at a conference in Istanbul in September 2003. The audience at that conference was mostly Muslim women, wearing their traditional coverings. Doyle Yager, the son of Dexter and Birdie Yager, was also one of the speakers from the United States. Merih and Nilufer Bolukbasi were our hosts.

United Kingdom

We traveled to London in May 2000 with my mother and sisters, Nana and Jean. Edna and I were guest speakers at two BWW seminars in the London area. At the first one, we were hosted by Rob and Babs Fee, the upline for our UK Amway business. At the second seminar, we had great fun with our hosts Pete and Lorraine Elliott. It was also good to see our friends Derek and Sue Smiley.

CHINA

Edna and I were in Guangzhou, China, for the Amway market launch in April 1995. Our downline Jun Bo Li met us in Guangzhou for the launch. Jun Bo Li and her husband,

John Hall, live in Cleveland and are in Dave and Theresa Mitchell's organization. Richard Montgomery, who was in Steve and Kym Taylor's organization, came over from the United States to join us for the launch, where we had great fun showing the business plan.

In China, we had to get used to the cars blowing their horns all the time. I asked someone, "Why does everybody blow their horns all the time?" and the reply came back: "If you hit someone and you blew your horn, then the accident is the other person's fault. But if you hit someone and you didn't blow your horn, then it's your fault." On one exciting ride, Richard Montgomery, Edna, and I were passengers in a taxi that got trapped between two buses on a circular road. The taxi driver and both bus drivers just sat in traffic and blew their horns. The three of us laughed and said, "We are not in the States anymore."

We had a great time at the launch with Phillip and Winnie Tong. The meetings were held in a school auditorium, and the bathrooms were missing at least one Western-style convenience: toilet paper. Fortunately, Winnie gave me a roll when I asked her where the restrooms were. In China, most bathrooms do not have toilet paper, and instead of a commode, many of them have just two imprints of feet on either side of a hole. Some have a brush and a pail of water for cleaning. Major hotels have Western-style commodes, and we learned to always use the bathroom before leaving the hotel! After the launch in Guangzhou, we spent three days in Hong Kong.

In May 1997, we were invited to speak in Beijing, Shanghai, and Hangzhou. Matthew Du was our host. While in Beijing, we saw the Forbidden City and had a private driver take us on a day tour to the Great Wall. Seeing these ancient sights was quite an experience.

We were invited to China to speak again in October 1998. On this trip, we spoke in Beijing, Huai Yin, Fuzhou, Nanjing, and Shanghai. Jose and Lucy Chang were our hosts and showed us a great time. In Huai Yin, the seminar was held at a movie theater. The attendance was larger than expected, and hundreds of people stood outside the theater. Government officials wanted to cancel the event, but they allowed us to speak for one hour. We met people who had traveled eight hours by train to meet us.

We, too, did a lot of train travel in China. On the ride from Nanjing to Shanghai, we traveled with Lucy and eight other IBOs. When the IBOs met new people on the train, they would bring their new friends to meet us and invite them to the seminar in Shanghai.

In Shanghai, we stayed at the Sheraton Hotel, where the food was delicious. After one meal with Lucy, I asked for some ice cream for dessert, but the waitress said that they didn't have any in the restaurant. The restaurant manager came over and offered to go to the gift shop in the hotel to get some ice cream. Lucy had been planning to take us sightseeing the next morning, but since she had a meeting to attend, she asked the manager to give us a tour instead. The next morning, the restaurant manager and our waitress, both of whom spoke English, took us around Shanghai by taxi. As we drove by the Shanghai Tower, I asked our guides if they had ever been to the revolving restaurant on top, but they said that it was too expensive for their budgets. To thank them for their kindness, Edna and I decided to treat them to lunch in the restaurant. Both young women were as excited as kids in a toy store as they took in the great view from the top of the Shanghai Tower. The restaurant had two buffets, one with traditional Chinese food and another with Western-style food. Both women filled their plates with chicken feet—a delicacy in China—and were surprised to learn that Edna also liked chicken feet. As for me, I enjoyed the chicken wings.

SOUTHEAST ASIA, AUSTRALIA, AND AFRICA

Australia

Edna and I had a great time in Sydney, Australia, in September 2010. We stayed at the beautiful Marriott Hotel downtown and celebrated our 39th wedding anniversary by visiting the Opera House area. All I can say is: WOW! Edna purchased a gold charm in the shape of the Opera House for her bracelet. We also visited the Australia Museum, which was quite interesting and educational. The food was delicious; Edna enjoyed the fish, and of course, I ate my share of chicken, along with fantastic desserts. We showed the business plan at the BWW open meeting in Sydney. Hemant and Smitha Sahela were our hosts. Everybody there wanted to know how to make money in an Internet business. One of the highlights of this trip was walking around Darling Harbor—with views that are among the most beautiful in the world. What a life!

India

We visited New Delhi in October 1998 and stayed at the Hyatt Regency Hotel. Ajay Gupta picked us up at the airport. Edna and I did home meetings for our downline A.K. and Chandni Sinha. They were internationally sponsored by their relatives Samyadev and Mala Datta in New Jersey and were a part of Darryl and Miriam Norton's group. A.K. and Chandni made us feel part of their family by putting *bindis* (red dots) on our foreheads. On one day of the trip, we took A.K. and Chandni and their team with us to the BWW seminar. Crown IBO Paul Miller from the United States was the guest speaker. We also took a day tour to Agra to see the Taj Mahal. As we approached the palace, we could see hundreds of people waiting to get in, but our tour driver pulled around to the back and entered through a hole in the gate. The driver walked us to the front of the line, showed his tour license, and we stepped right in to this wonder of the world.

Malaysia

Edna and I traveled to Kuala Lumpur in January 2003. We were invited by BWW to be the guest speakers at a Winter Conference at the Mandarin Oriental Hotel. S.F. and Celia Wong were our hosts and took us sightseeing in this beautiful city. Among other attractions, we saw the Petronas Towers, which are twin buildings, 88 floors high, with a bridge connecting the two on the 41st and 42nd floors. It was quite an impressive structure.

New Zealand

In September 2010, Edna and I had a great trip to Auckland, staying at the Hilton at Prince Wharf. From our balcony room, we had a lovely view of the harbor. Highlights of our trip included a tour of the Auckland Museum, attendance at a special Maori cultural experience with haka dancing, and a ferryboat ride to Devonport. There, we walked through the shopping area near the harbor and had lunch. On Queen Street Edna purchased a beautiful jacket made of possum with merino wool, a special fabric in New Zealand. The food in New Zealand was great, too. One night, we went to a Korean barbeque buffet, where the food was cooked at the table while diners were entertained by a band and dancers. The best meal we ate during the trip was at the Euro restaurant, just down the street from the Hilton. We both had our favorites: broiled salmon for Edna and rotisserie chicken for me. For dessert, we sampled a creme brulee trio with three favors, lemon, coffee, and strawberry.

The Philippines

We were invited by BWW to be the guest speakers at seminars in Manila, Cebu City, and Davao City in the Philippines in May 1997. We were met there by our downline Tracy and Zena Adams, who now live in Maryland, although Zena is originally from the Philippines. In Manila, we stayed at the beautiful Shangri-La Hotel. In the restaurant of the hotel, I got my first taste of fresh-squeezed mango juice; afterwards, I had mango juice and golden mangos every day. After a great seminar in Manila, we traveled to Cebu City and stayed at the Marriott. Zena grow up in Cebu City and had many relatives there. Our last stop in the Philippines was in Davao City. We stayed at a beautiful hotel on the beach where the seminar was held.

Singapore

We traveled to Singapore to stay at a Marriott and speak at a BWW seminar in January 2003. After the seminar, we spent four days enjoying the country, with Chew Teik Huat as our host.

South Africa

Edna and I were invited by BWW to be the guest speakers at seminars in Johannesburg, Cape Town, and Durbin in March 1999. Rod Moodie was our host, and we had a wonderful time in all three locations. Our downline Darryl and Miriam Norton and Leo Pickett were in South Africa for the market launch in 1997. We had a home meeting for Norton's downline Minnie, and we met with Leo's downline Shoneeze Sarjoo. Shoneeze is the daughter of Basil and Sherrene Van Der Merwe, who were living in the Washington, DC, area at the time.

Thailand

In October 1998, Edna and I visited Bangkok and showed the business plan at the open meeting for Smaron and Luck Komolavanij. Smaron is the nephew of Susie Loewecke, who lives in Maryland with her husband, Don. In Bangkok, we stayed at the Hyatt Regency Hotel and had a fun time with Smaron and Luck. One of the most memorable experiences was our visit to the Grand Palace, a complex of beautiful gold buildings in the heart of Bangkok.

Chapter 7

JUST HAVE FUN!

—◦◦◦—

As you go through life, of course, you will encounter problems. This chapter presents techniques I use to stay positive in the face of problems and to keep on having fun. When I speak at a seminar, my objective is to stop talking before the audience stops listening. I always plan to end my speech a few minutes before the scheduled time to keep the audience looking for more. I also like to make the audience repeat aloud the important points in my speech and tell them a lot of jokes. I've found that if I can keep the audience laughing with me, then I have them in the palm of my hand. You might say something similar about problems you face in life: If you can keep your sense of humor when you face a problem, you have control over it and can find a solution.

Keep a positive attitude.

One of my favorite attitude jokes is about a man who was driving all night. As the sun came up, he decided to stop and get some breakfast. He walked into an all-night café and was met at the door by the waitress. He could tell that she had been up all night by her attitude. In a rough voice, she said, "Follow me" and walked the man to a table. Then, she dropped the menu on the table and walked away. After he looked at the menu, the man tried to figure out a way to make the waitress smile. She came back to take his order and said, "What do you want?" The man replied, "Give me two eggs over light and a few kind words." The waitress wrote down the order and headed into the kitchen. A few minutes later, she reappeared and dropped the eggs in front of her customer. He said, "Ok, here are the eggs, but where are the kind words?" The waitress replied, "Don't eat those eggs."

Be patient with people.

This joke was a favorite of my best friend, Horace Harris. Edna and I will always miss Horace, who passed away in 2008. We are so proud of his wife, Constance, for keeping his dream alive for so many people. In this joke, a man with his dog stops at an outdoor café to have lunch with a friend. As the two are having lunch, the dog starts making a painful groaning sound: "Urr urr." The friend tries to ignore the noise, but the dog keeps making the sound: "Urr urr." Finally, the friend asks, "What's wrong with your dog?" The man looks over at the dog and says, "He's sitting on a nail." The friend says, "Why doesn't he move?" "Well," comes the reply, "it's not hurting him bad enough." I think about this joke when I show people our business plan and hear them say, "Urr urr." I know that their financial situation is not hurting them bad enough.

Are you moving fast?

A fellow who just bought a new sports car was driving

on a rural highway to see how fast the car would go. As he was speeding along, he noticed a three-legged chicken pass him by. The man sped up to catch the chicken, and again, the chicken pulled away. Then, the man noticed that the chicken pulled off the highway to a small farm. He followed it to the farm and asked the farmer about the three-legged chicken. The farmer told the man that he, his wife, and his daughter all liked chicken legs, so he bred a special three-legged chicken to make sure every one could get a leg. The man asked, "How does the chicken taste?" and the farmer replied, "I don't know; we haven't been able to catch one yet!"

You can do it.

This joke is the favorite of Dave and Jan Severn, who went Diamond with Edna and I in 1981. Jan passed away in 2011 and is missed. I told this joke at the Portland, Oregon, FED for Ron and Georgia Lee Puryear organization World Wide. The building that housed an insurance company in a small, rural town caught on fire. The local fire department tried but couldn't put out the fire. The president of the insurance company called the fire chief in the next town and offered him $1,000 if his men could come and put out the fire. As the fire truck came into town, it didn't even stop; it just went straight into the building. The hoses shot water everywhere, and in a few minutes, the fire was out. The fire chief emerged from the building covered with smoke, and the president of the insurance company said, "That was the most incredible job I've ever seen. I'm not just going to give you $1,000, but I'm going to give you $2,000 for that job." The president wrote the check for $2,000 and gave it to the fire chief, whose eyes lit up.

The president asked, "What are you going to do with that check?" And the fire chief said, "The first thing I'm going to do is get the brakes fixed on that truck."

Smile and make a new friend.

I've set a goal to meet someone new every day, and Paul Miller gave me the simple secret for meeting new people: Get out of your house. I take Paul's advice and go places, like the bank, the post office, and stores, where I will find people. When I'm walking along or waiting in line, I smile and speak first to anyone who's nearby. A smile will open doors for you. Keep it simple and say hi. If someone says hi back, then start a conversation. That kind of meeting is one of what I call the easy ones. Just look for people who seem friendly. If you keep meeting people, you will eventually find Bubba, the person who knows every important person in the world.

One day, Bubba's friend said to Bubba, "You cannot know every important person in the world." Bubba replied, "Yes, I do." His friend shook his head and said, "You don't know an actor (you select the actor)." "Sure, I know that actor," Bubba said, so they went to Beverly Hills and drove to the actor's home. Bubba and his friend rang the doorbell, and the butler answered and said, "They are in the backyard, cooking out." When Bubba and his friend went around back, the actor looked up and said, "Hey, Bubba." His friend said, "I can't believe it, but you know that actor," and Bubba said, "I told you I know every important person in the world."

"What about the President of the United States?" Bubba's friend asked. "You don't know him." Bubba said, "Sure, I know the President." So the two traveled to Washington, DC, and went to the White House. After they passed through security, the doors of the Oval Office opened, and the President said, "Hey, Bubba." His friend said, "I can't believe it, but you know the President of the United States," and Bubba said, "I told you I know every important person in the world."

Finally, Bubba's friend said, "You absolutely cannot know the Pope." Again, Bubba said that he did, and the two were off to Italy. The Pope was on a platform speaking to a large crowd. Bubba said, "Stand here and I will go on the platform with the Pope." His friend watched Bubba work his way through the crowd and climb up on the platform. The Pope turned around and said, "Hey, Bubba," at which point, the friend fainted. Bubba worked his way back through the crowd and shook his friend to wake him. "Are you all right?" Bubba asked. His friend opened his eyes and said, "I was doing Ok until the fellow next to me said, 'Who's that up there with Bubba?'"

Chapter 8

MY "SECRETS OF SUCCESS"

——∿∿——

M ost people are looking for their niche in life—the place where they are comfortable, can make a reasonable living, and be happy. When I first encountered the Amway business, I didn't realize that it would be my niche. I've since learned that the key to finding your niche is to look for something you enjoy and believe in and then have fun doing it. The more I built my Amway business, the more I enjoyed it and and built it with honesty. What I like about Amway is that it is a business for all people. No matter what your race or religion is, you are treated with respect for who you are. As a Black man, I have spoken all over the world to a variety of people, and they have all treated Edna and me like family. When you are successful and you are trying to help others in the business be successful, they do not care what color you are. I am a Christian, but there are all types of religions in the business. We respect people for who they are. One Sunday morning in 2011, at a BWW event in Richmond, VA, seven worship services were held: non-denominational Christian, Buddhist, Jewish, Zoroastrian, Hindu, Muslim, and Sikh.

Two of my other secrets to success are equally simple: to keep your body and your mind fit.

Keeping Your Body Fit

Of course, we all know the importance of physical health. I would recommend that you get a physical exam at least once a year or, depending on your situation, perhaps twice a year. Because high blood pressure runs in my family, I make it a point to see my doctor, Dr. Michael Mitchell, every six months. Like most people, I don't always eat three well-balanced meals a day, so I also take a multivitamin, another practice you might want to consider. I also have glaucoma, which is high pressure in my eyes, another condition that runs in my family. Both my mother and my sisters use the same eye drops to control their glaucoma. I see my eye doctor, Dr. Kenneth Karlin, every three to four months to make sure the pressure in my eyes is at the right level. Another suggestion is to see your dentist regularly. One of the best investments I've made was to purchase dental insurance, which allows me to visit my dentist, Dr. Parvin Amouhashem, every four months to get my teeth cleaned.

Edna and I do not smoke cigarettes or drink alcohol. I stopped drinking any alcohol more than 30 years ago. We do not even drink wine with dinner. At a leadership meeting I attended, Bill Britt spoke about how alcohol affects your judgment, which is why no alcohol is served at any of the BWW meetings. I agree with what Bill said, so I'm glad to be a designated driver!

Find yourself an exercise program that you will be consistent with. Some people like going to the gym, jogging, or walking. I do some sit-ups and push-ups every morning and evening, and it's easy for me to walk 30 minutes every day. I live within about a 15-minute walk of my bank, post office, and a store. By the time I do my errands and walk back home, I've done my 30 minutes.

Keeping Your Mind Fit

To maintain my mental health, I take 15 to 20 minutes every morning to read and pray. As with exercising your body, it's important to find a routine for exercising your mind that you like and can be consistent with. Here is my morning routine:

1) I read *The One Year Bible*, which is the entire King James Version arranged in 365 daily readings. By the end of the year, I have read the whole Bible, and then I start again.

2) I read the chapter in Proverbs that corresponds with the day of the month. This was an idea I got from Paul Miller, who mentioned at a leadership meeting that Proverbs has 31 chapters, which makes it a natural for reading a chapter a day.

3) I read my own personal version of the prayer of Jabez. The prayer of Jabez is from 1 Chronicles 4:10: "And Ja'-bez called on the God of Israel, saying, Oh that thou wouldest bless me indeed, and enlarge my coast, and that thine hand might be with me, and that thou wouldest keep me from evil, that it may not grieve me! And God granted him that which he requested." To learn more about this passage, I recommend you read *The Prayer of Jabez* by Bruce Wilkinson.

4) I keep a list of Bible scriptures that I read in the morning, as follows:

Matthew 6:9–13

9 After this manner therefore pray ye: Our Father which art in heaven, Hallowed be thy name.

10 Thy kingdom come. Thy will be done in earth, as it is in heaven.

11 Give us this day our daily bread.

12 And forgive us our debts, as we forgive our debtors.

13 And lead us not into temptation, but deliver us from evil: For thine is the kingdom, and the power, and the glory, for ever.

A-men.

Psalm 23:1–6

1 The Lord is my shepherd; I shall not want.

2 He maketh me to lie down in green pastures; he leadeth me beside the still waters.

3 He restoreth my soul: he leadeth me in the paths of righteousness for his name sake.

4 Yea, though I walk through the valley of the shadow of death, I will fear no evil: for thou art with me; thy rod and thy staff they comfort me.

5 Thou preparest a table before me in the presence of mine enemies: thou anointest my head with oil; my cup runneth over.

6 Surely goodness and mercy shall follow me all the days of my life: and I will dwell in the house of the Lord for ever.

Mark 11:24

Therefore, I say unto you, What things soever ye desire, when ye pray, believe that ye receive them, and ye shall have them.

3 John 1:2

Beloved, I wish above all things that thou mayest prosper and be in health, even as thy soul prospereth.

Philippians 4:13

I can do all things through Christ which strengtheneth me.

5) Napoleon Hill's book *Think and Grow Rich* inspired me to write down and date my goals. Now, I keep an index card with my goals written on it that I read every day. I also read a daily motivational statement from a booklet called "A gift for each day ...." The booklet was a Christmas gift in 1985 from Diamonds John and Bobbi Sestina.

6) I read the "Eight Magic Words" from the book *Winning without Intimidation* by Bob Burg. These Eight Magic Words will generally prompt others to try their best to help you. Try these for starters: "If you can't do it, I'll definitely understand," followed by "If you can, I'd certainly appreciate it." If it's appropriate, you can add the words "I don't want you to get yourself in hot water over it."

7) I read the ten powerful phases *Ten Powerful Phases for Positive People* by Rich DeVos. These phrases are: I'm Wrong, I'm Sorry, You Can Do It, I Believe in You, I'm Proud of You, Thank You, I Need You, I Trust You, I Respect You, and I Love You.

8) I read the seven habits from Stephen R. Covey's *7 Habits of Highly Effective People*:

Habit 1 – Be Proactive: The habit of being proactive, or the habit of personal vision, means taking responsibility for our attitudes and actions.

Habit 2 – Begin with the End in Mind: This is the habit of personal leadership. Start with a clear destination to understand where you are now, where you're going and what you value most.

Habit 3 – Put First Things First: This is the habit of personal management, which involves organizing and managing time and events. Manage yourself. Organize and execute around priorities.

Habit 4 – Think Win/Win: Win/Win is the habit of interpersonal leadership. Win/Win is the attitude of seeking mutual benefit. This thinking begins with a commitment to explore all options until a mutually satisfactory solution is reached, or to make no deal at all.

Habit 5 – Seek First to Understand…Then to be Understood: This is the habit of empathic communication. Understanding builds the skill of empathic listening that inspires openness and trust.

Habit 6 – Synergize: This is the habit creative cooperation or teamwork. Synergy results from valuing differences by bringing different perspectives together in the spirit of mutual respect.

Habit 7 – Sharpen the Saw: This is the habit of self-renewal. Preserving and enhancing your greatest asset, yourself, by renewing the physical, spiritual, mental and social/emotional dimensions of your nature.

9) I read Ruben's Rules for Success and the Champion's Creed from the book *The Courage to Succeed* by Ruben Gonzalez.

Ruben's Rules for Success:

1. You will never achieve anything great in life until you start to believe that something inside you is bigger than the circumstances you face.
2. You can become great by making a decision to pursue your dream in life and by refusing to quit.
3. Every success you're ever had or will ever have is the product of your courage to act and the courage to endure.
4. Success is not about how much talent you have. It's about what you do with the talent you do have.
5. Successful people love the battle, the challenge and the journey. It's about knowing that you did your best.
6. If you do whatever it takes for however long it takes, success is only a matter of time.

The Champion's Creed:

I am a champion.
I believe in myself.
I have the will to win.
I set high goals for myself.
I surround myself with winners.
I'm cool, positive, and confident.
I'm willing to pay the price of success.
I stay relaxed and in control at all times.
I focus all my energy on the job at hand.
I take responsibility for all of my results.
I have the courage to endure and persist.
I vividly imagine what victory will feel like.
I am a champion and I will win.

Gonzalez suggests that you read this creed every morning with passion to have a better and more productive day. You can print a copy at www.thechampionscreed. com. All I can say is, it has been working for me.

10) I end the session with a prayer.

My Wish for You

I hope this book helps you to focus on your dream. Just remember that achieving your dream will take work, but you can make it fun work. As I traveled the world in every country, I noticed that traffic lights mean the same thing. If the light is red, you stop; if it is yellow, you slow down and proceed with caution; and if it is green, you go. For you right now, the light is green. That means GO for your dream.

Pictures

———～—

If you would like to view some of the pictures in this book in color, visit www.itisfunmakingmoney.com.

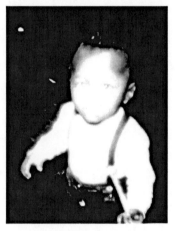

G.W. Jr. as a baby

G.W. Jr. as a boy

Nana, G.W. Sr., Vivian, G.W. Jr., Edith and Jean in 1955

G.W. Sr., Edith, Vivian, Edna, G.W. Jr., Andrea, Nana and Jean

Grandmother Josephine King, Edna, G.W. Jr., Grandmother Rosie Blair

Rosie, Edith, Denny, Peaches, Sis and Rosemary

Daddy Adams and son Wayne with big catfish

97

Edna, Bruce, Dianna, Steve, Lori, Uncle Carl, Deborah,
Wayne, Larry and Mama Adams

Peaches, G.W. Jr. & Edith in Moscow, Russia

G.W. Jr., Edith, Edna and G.W. Sr. in Caracas, Venezuela

Edna and G.W. in Accra, Ghana

Jean, Edith, Nana, Edna and G.W. in Paris, France

G.W. and Edna at the Coliseum in Rome, Italy

President Reagan, Edna and G.W.
Courtesy Ronald Reagan Library

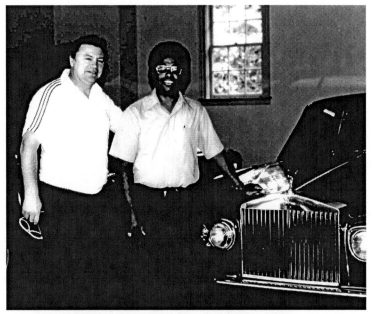

Bill Britt and G.W. in front of Bill's Rolls Royce

Edna and G.W. in Venice, Italy

G.W. & Edna at the Taj Mahal in Agra, India

Edna and G.W. at the Grand Palace in Bangkok, Thailand

G.W. on the Great Wall of China

Edna, Edith, Jean, Nana and G.W. in London, England

G.W. and Edna at the Opera House in Sidney, Australia

Jessica, Andrea, Arielle, Edna and G.W. in Madrid, Spain